*Here's what people are saying about*
*the* DOING LIFE TOGETHER

D1413073

## Small Group Members Are Saying...

Six weeks ago we were strangers. Today we are a family in Christ. We talk to each other, lean on each other, encourage each other, and hold each other accountable. We have gone from meeting as a Bible study to getting together for several social events, meeting for Sunday services, and organizing service projects in our community.

—Sandy and Craig

The Purpose-Driven material quickly moved us beyond group and closer toward family, beyond reading God's Word to knowing God!

—The Coopers

## Small Group Leaders Are Saying...

Even though our group has been together for several years, the questions in this study have allowed us to connect on a much deeper level. Many of the men are displaying emotions we haven't seen before.

—Steve and Jennifer

The material has become a personal compass to me. When I find myself needing to make a decision, I ask, "Does it bring me closer to God's family? Does it make me more like Christ? Am I using the gifts God gave me? Am I sharing God's love? Am I surrendering my life to please God?" I still have a long way to go, but this has been a blessing and a compass to keep me on his path.

—Craig

## Pastors and Church Leaders Are Saying...

We took the entire church through this curriculum, and the results were nothing less than miraculous. Our congregation was ignited with passion for God and his purposes for our lives. It warmed up the entire congregation as we grew closer to God by "Doing Life Together."

—Kerry

The Purpose-Driven format helped our groups realize there are some areas that they are doing very well in (fellowship and discipleship) and other areas that they need to do some work in. What is amazing is to see how they are committing to work on these areas (especially evangelism and ministry).

—Steve

# Other Studies in the DOING LIFE TOGETHER Series

After you complete this study, we'd love to hear how DOING LIFE TOGETHER has affected your life, your group, or your church! Write us at stories@lifetogether.com. You can also log on to www.lifetogether.com to see how others are putting "life together" into practice.

# SHARING YOUR
# LIFE MISSION EVERY DAY

six sessions on
*evangelism*

written by
BRETT and DEE EASTMAN
TODD and DENISE WENDORFF
KAREN LEE-THORP

GRAND RAPIDS, MICHIGAN 49530 USA

We want to hear from you. Please send your comments about this book to us in care of the address below. Thank you.

GRAND RAPIDS, MICHIGAN 49530 USA

WWW.ZONDERVAN.COM

ZONDERVAN™

*Sharing Your Life Mission Every Day*
Copyright © 2002 by Brett and Deanna Eastman, Todd and Denise Wendorff,
and Karen Lee-Thorp

Requests for information should be addressed to:
Zondervan, *Grand Rapids, Michigan 49530*

ISBN 0-310-24676-8

*Interior icons by Tom Clark*

*Printed in the United States of America*

02 03 04 05 06 07 08 /❖ DC/ 10 9 8 7 6 5 4 3

# CONTENTS

# FOREWORD

Over twenty-five years ago I noticed a little phrase in Acts 13:36 that forever altered the direction of my life. It read, *"David had served God's purpose in his own generation."* I was fascinated by that simple yet profound summary of David's life, and I determined to make it the goal of my life, too. I would seek to discover and fulfill the purposes for which God had created me.

This decision provoked a number of questions: What are God's purposes for putting us on earth? What does a purpose-driven life look like? How can the church enable people to fulfill God's eternal purposes? I read through the Bible again and again, searching for the answers to these questions. As a direct result of what I learned, my wife, Kay, and I decided to start Saddleback Church and build it from the ground up on God's five purposes for us (which are found in the New Testament).

In the living laboratory of Saddleback Church, we were able to experiment with different ways to help people understand, apply, and live out the purposes of God. I've written two books about the lessons we've learned (*The Purpose-Driven Church* and, more recently, *The Purpose-Driven Life*). As other churches became interested in what we were doing, we began sharing the tools, programs, and studies we developed at Saddleback. Over a million copies of *The Purpose-Driven Church* are now in print in some nineteen languages, and The Purpose-Driven Class Curriculum (Class 101–401) is now used in tens of thousands of churches around the world. We hope that the same will be true for this exciting new small group curriculum.

DOING LIFE TOGETHER is a groundbreaking study in several ways. It is the first small group curriculum built completely on the purpose-driven paradigm. This is not just another study to be used *in* your church; it is a study *on* the church to help *strengthen* your church. Many small group curricula today are quite self-focused and individualistic. They generally do not address the importance of the local church and our role in it as believers. Another unique feature of this curriculum is its balance. In every session, the five purposes of God are stressed in some way.

But the greatest reason I am excited about releasing this DOING LIFE TOGETHER curriculum is that I've seen the dramatic changes it produces in the lives of those who study it. These small group studies were not developed in some detached ivory tower or academic setting but in the day-to-day ministry of Saddleback Church, where thousands of people meet weekly in small groups that are committed to fulfilling God's purposes. This curriculum has been tested and retested, and the results have been absolutely amazing. Lives have been changed, marriages saved, and families strengthened. And our church has grown—in the past seven years we've seen over 9,100 new believers baptized at Saddleback. I attribute these results to the fact that so many of our members are serious about living healthy, balanced, purpose-driven lives.

It is with great joy and expectation that I introduce this resource to you. I am so proud of our development team on this project: Brett and Dee Eastman, Todd and Denise Wendorff, and Karen Lee-Thorp. They have committed hundreds of hours to write, teach, develop, and refine these lessons —with much feedback along the way. This has been a labor of love, as they have shared our dream of helping you serve God's purpose in your own generation. The church will be enriched for eternity as a result.

Get ready for a life-changing journey. God bless!

—Pastor Rick Warren

Pastor Rick Warren is the author of *The Purpose-Driven Church* and *The Purpose-Driven Life* [www.purposedrivenlife.com].

# ACKNOWLEDGMENTS

Sometimes in life God gives you a dream. Most of the time it remains only a dream. But every once in a while, a dream captures your heart, consumes your thoughts, and compels you to action. However, if others around you aren't motivated to share the dream and aren't moved to action along with you, it remains just that—a dream. By the grace of God and a clear call on the hearts of a few, our dream has become a reality.

The DOING LIFE TOGETHER series was birthed one summer in the hearts of Brett and Dee Eastman and Todd and Denise Wendorff, two Saddleback Church staff couples. They hoped to launch a new one-year Bible study based on the Purpose-Driven® life. They called it *The Journey: Experiencing the Transformed Life*. *The Journey* was launched with a leadership team that committed its heart and soul to the project. We will never be able to express our gratitude to each of you who shared the dream and helped to continue the dream now, three years later.

Early on, Karen Lee-Thorp, an experienced writer of many Bible studies, joined the team. Oh, God, you are good to us!

Saddleback pastors and staff members too numerous to mention have supported our dream and have come alongside to fan the flames. We would have never gotten this off the ground without their belief and support.

We also want to express our overwhelming gratitude to the numerous ministries and churches that helped shape our spiritual heritage. We're particularly grateful for Bill Bright of Campus Crusade for Christ, who gave us a dream for reaching the world, and for Bill Hybels of Willow Creek Community Church, who gave us a great love and respect for the local church.

Our special thanks goes to Pastor Rick and Kay Warren for sharing the dream of a healthy and balanced purpose-driven church that produces purpose-driven lives over time. It clearly is the basis for the body of this work. God only knows how special you are to us and how blessed we feel to be a part of your team.

Finally, we thank our beloved families who have lived with us, laughed at us, and loved us through it all. We love doing our lives together with you.

# DOING LIFE TOGETHER

Doing Life Together is unique in that it was designed in community for community. Four of us have been doing life together, in one way or another, for over fifteen years. We have been in a small group together, done ministry together, and been deeply involved in each other's lives. We have shared singleness, marriage, childbirth, family loss, physical ailments, teenage years, job loss, and, yes, even marital problems.

Our community has not been perfect, but it has been real. We have made each other laugh beyond belief, cry to the point of exhaustion, feel as grateful as one can imagine, and get so mad we couldn't see straight. We've said things we will always regret and shared moments we will never forget, but through it all we have discovered a diamond in the rough—a community that increasingly reflects the character of Jesus Christ. God has used our relationships with each other to deepen our understanding of and intimacy with him. We have come to believe that we cannot fully experience the breadth and depth of the purpose-driven life outside of loving relationships in the family of God (Ephesians 2:19–22; 4:11–13).

Doing life together was God's plan from the beginning of time. From the relationships of Father, Son, and Holy Spirit in the Trinity, to the twelve apostles, to the early house churches, and even Jesus' final words in the Great Commission (Matthew 28:16–20)—all share the pattern of life together. God longs to connect all of his children in loving relationships that cultivate the five biblical purposes of the church deep within their hearts. With this goal in mind, we have created the Doing Life Together series—the first purpose-driven small group series.

The series is designed to walk you and your group down a path, six weeks at a time over the course of a year, to help you do the purpose-driven life together. There are six study guides in this series. You can study them individually, or you can follow the one-year path through the six studies. *Beginning Life Together* offers a six-week overview of the purpose-driven life. The other five guides (*Connecting with God's Family, Growing to Be Like Christ, Developing Your SHAPE to Serve Others, Sharing Your Life Mission Every Day,* and *Surrendering Your Life for God's Pleasure*) each explore one of the five purposes of the church more deeply.

In his book *The Purpose-Driven Life*, Rick Warren invites you to commit to live a purpose-driven life every day. The DOING LIFE TOGETHER series was designed to help you live this purpose-driven life through being part of a purpose-driven small group. A purpose-driven group doesn't simply connect people in community or grow people through Bible study. These groups seek to help each member balance all five biblical purposes of the church. The fivefold purpose of a healthy group parallels the fivefold purpose of the church.

## Widening the Circle

Some Christians struggle with sharing their faith because they think they're on their own. Sharing your life mission every day is so much easier when it grows out of your life together with God and his family. Take Donna and Paul, for example. Their small group decided to attend church together one Sunday morning. Donna and others noticed a woman sitting nearby. She had a hospital band on her wrist, and she was crying. Donna and Paul saw an opportunity to care. They introduced themselves and asked about the hospital band. The woman explained that she had given birth to a stillborn baby girl just a few days before. She and her husband weren't churchgoers, but they had felt so miserable at home that morning that they had decided to visit Saddleback Church.

Soon the whole small group was listening. Two members prayed for the couple. Each day for the next week three group members took them meals. The couple began to attend church regularly, and another friend took them to a grief support group. As time went on, every member took steps to care in his or her own way. Months later, the couple made a decision to follow Jesus Christ and be baptized. Today they belong to a small group full of young couples. They are moving forward, putting their hope in Jesus, because Donna and Paul's group was open to an opportunity to draw outsiders into their life together.

This is what sharing your faith is all about—widening the circle of your life with God and God's family to welcome outsiders. It's living your life together so fully that outsiders want in. It's astonishing your neighbor by loving her as well as you love yourself. And yes, it's knowing how to answer curious questions when they come up and how to help a person commit her life to Jesus Christ when she is ready.

If life with God is the best thing that's ever happened to you, you'll spread it around. Nothing will draw you deeper into the heart of God than feeling his heartbeat for those who don't yet know him. Nothing will draw your group of Christian friends together more than when you turn your eyes outward. Want more life? Give it away!

## Outline of Each Session

Most people desire to live a purpose-driven life, but few people actually achieve this on a consistent basis. That's why we've included elements of the five purposes in every meeting—so that you can live a healthy, balanced spiritual life over time.

When you see the following symbols in this book, you will know that the questions and exercises in that section promote that particular purpose.

 **CONNECTING** WITH GOD'S FAMILY (FELLOWSHIP). The foundation for spiritual growth is an intimate connection with God and his family. The questions in this section will help you get to know the members of your small group so that you'll begin to feel a sense of belonging. This section is designed to open your time together and provide a fun way to share your personal stories with one another.

 **GROWING** TO BE LIKE CHRIST (DISCIPLESHIP). This is the most exciting portion of each lesson. Each week you'll study one or two core passages from the Bible. The focus will be on how the truths from God's Word make a difference in your lives. We will often provide an experiential exercise to enable you not just to talk about the truth but also to experience it in a practical way.

 **DEVELOPING** YOUR SHAPE TO SERVE OTHERS (MINISTRY). Most people want to know how God has uniquely shaped them for ministry and where they can serve in the center of his will. This section will help make that desire a reality.

 **SHARING** YOUR LIFE MISSION EVERY DAY (EVANGELISM). Many people skip over this aspect of the Christian life because it's scary, relationally awkward, or simply too much work for their busy schedules. We understand, because we have these thoughts as well. But God calls all of us to reach out a hand to people who don't know him. It's much easier to take practical, manageable steps that can be integrated naturally into everyday life if you take them together. Every week you will have an opportunity to take a small step.

 **SURRENDERING** YOUR LIFE FOR GOD'S PLEASURE (WORSHIP). A surrendered heart is what pleases God most. Each small group session will give you a chance to surrender your heart to God and one another in prayer. In addition, you'll be introduced to several forms of small group worship, including listening to worship CDs, singing together, reading psalms, and participating in Communion. This portion of your meeting will transform your life in ways you never thought possible. If you're new to praying in a small group, you won't be pressed to pray aloud until you feel ready.

**STUDY NOTES.** This section provides background notes on the Bible passage(s) you examine in the GROWING section. You may want to refer to these notes during your study.

**FOR FURTHER STUDY.** This section can help your more spiritually mature members take the session one step further each week on their own. If your group is ready for deeper study or is comfortable doing homework, this section and the following two sections will help you get there. You may want to encourage them to read these passages and reflect on them in a personal journal or in the Notes section at the end of each session.

**MEMORY VERSES.** For those group members who want to take a step of hiding God's Word in their hearts, there are six memory verses on page 80 that correspond to each weekly lesson. You may want to tear out this page and cut the verses into wallet- or purse-size cards for easy access.

**PURPOSE-DRIVEN LIFE READING PLAN.** This plan for reading *The Purpose-Driven Life* by Rick Warren parallels the weekly sessions in this study guide. *The Purpose-Driven Life* is the perfect complement to the DOING LIFE TOGETHER series. If your group wants to apply the material taught in the book, you can simply read the recommended piece each week, write a reflection, and discuss the teaching as a group or in pairs.

**DAILY DEVOTIONS.** One of the easiest ways for your group to grow together is to encourage each other to read God's Word on a regular basis. It's so much easier to stay motivated in this area if you have one another's support. On page 81 is a daily reading plan that parallels the study and helps you deepen your walk with God. There are five readings per week. If you really want to grow, we suggest you pair up with a friend (spiritual partner) to encourage each other throughout the week. Decide right now, and write the name of someone you'd like to join with for the next six weeks.

# GOD'S HEART FOR PEOPLE

Have you ever longed for one of your friends to come to know God but you didn't know how to help? I know a young man who claims to be uninterested in God. At age nineteen he told me, "I don't believe in God. I don't need to. I don't want to." His life is just fine, thank you. He's smart and looking for a career that will let him express his creativity and buy him life's pleasures.

When I offered him the gospel, he slammed the door in my face. My first reaction was to feel hurt and back away. But he's an important person in my life. I keep seeing his face in my prayers. Underneath his talent and bravado, I sense a thirsty heart. I'm convinced that God aches to embrace him, and I suspect that God has a long-range plan to pursue his heart. When I feel God ache for my friend, my own heart melts.

God's plan may take years to unfold. I may have only the tiniest role in it. But when I let myself share God's heart for my friend, I know I can't give up on him.

—Karen

## CONNECTING WITH GOD'S FAMILY                                    10 min.

Few people decide to follow Jesus on their own. For most of us, one or more people are influential in our decision. They may be friends, relatives, even writers of books. They may be people we know well or people we admire at a distance.

Please share your answer to question 1 below. Try to limit your story to about a minute so we'll have plenty of time for the rest of the study.

1. When you decided to follow Jesus, who was one person who influenced your decision? How did he or she influence you?

2. It's important for every group to agree on a set of shared values. If your group doesn't already have an agreement (sometimes called a covenant), turn to page 67. Even if you've been together for some time and your values are clear, the Purpose-Driven Group Agreement can help your group achieve greater health and balance. We recommend that you especially consider rotating group leadership, setting up spiritual partners, and introducing purpose teams into the group. Simply go over the values and expectations listed in the agreement to be sure everyone in the group understands and accepts them. Make any necessary decisions about such issues as refreshments and child care.

## GROWING TO BE LIKE CHRIST                                    20 min.

Just as someone helped you begin your journey with Jesus, our Lord offers you a unique opportunity to play this same role in the lives of others around you. The first step is to see people as Jesus saw them—distressed and downcast, like sheep without a shepherd. We tend to see people as they appear on the outside, unaware of the needs that lie below the surface. We need to look deeper and develop a heart for people in need of a savior.

> *Jesus went through all the towns and villages, teaching in their synagogues, preaching the good news of the kingdom and healing every disease and sickness. 36When he saw the crowds, he had compassion on them, because they were harassed and helpless, like sheep without a shepherd. 37Then he said to his disciples, "The harvest is plentiful but the workers are few. 38Ask the Lord of the harvest, therefore, to send out workers into his harvest field."*
>
> —Matthew 9:35–38

**3.** What did Jesus see and feel as he visited the cities and villages around him?

*Helpless/lost people ... needing guidance. He felt much work needed to be done.*

**4.** Read the definition of *compassion* in the study notes on page 21. Why do you think Jesus had compassion on the people?

Why wouldn't they have been fine with a little rest, food, and direction?

**5.** Jesus said that these people ultimately needed a "shepherd." What do you think he meant by that?

**6.** What did Jesus mean by his statement that "the harvest is plentiful but the workers are few"?

7. Whom do you know who seems like a sheep without a shepherd? How does this person's situation make you feel?

8. Think of someone you know who doesn't believe in God and yet doesn't appear to be "harassed and helpless." Why do you think Jesus feels compassion for this person?

9. Jesus is the shepherd people need (John 10:11). Why do we sometimes neglect people's deepest needs?

Sometimes the tyranny of the urgent robs us from the real work that God wants each of us to take part in. The German poet Goethe wrote, "The things that matter most must never be at the mercy of the things that matter least."

## SHARING YOUR LIFE MISSION EVERY DAY          20 min.

Compassion doesn't come naturally for everyone. Jesus wants you to develop the kind of compassion for people that he has.

10. Who are the sheep without a shepherd in your life, the people who need to meet Jesus? The following "Circles of Life" will help you think of people in various areas of your life. Prayerfully write down at least three or four names in the circles.

### Circles of Life

Family
(immediate or extended)

Acquaintances
(neighbors, kids' sports teams, school, and so forth)

Friends

Fun
(gym, hobbies, hangouts)

Work

11. Share one or two names with the group. Together write down a Top Ten list—the names of the ten unbelievers your group will pray for during the next six weeks.

| Top Ten List |
| --- |
| |
| |
| |
| |
| |
| |
| |
| |
| |
| |

**SURRENDERING** YOUR LIFE FOR GOD'S PLEASURE  15–30 min.

Compassion flows out of your intimate connection with Jesus, your shepherd. If you're harassed and helpless yourself, you're hardly likely to be thinking about the needs of other sheep. Here are some ways you can strengthen your connection with Jesus.

12. On page 81 you'll find a list of brief passages for daily devotions—five per week for the six weeks of this study. If you've never spent daily time with God, this is an easy way to begin. Would you consider taking on this habit for the duration of this study? See page 84 for a sample journal page that you can use as a guide for your daily devotions.

  If you're already consistent in daily devotions, consider acquiring the habit of Scripture memory. Six memory verses are provided on page 80—one verse per week. Would you consider accepting the challenge to memorize one verse per week and hide God's Word in your heart? We urge you to pair up with another person for encouragement and accountability.

**13.** Allow everyone to answer this question: "How can we pray for you this week?"

Take some time to pray for these requests. Pray also for the people on your Top Ten list. Ask God to prepare their hearts for the gospel and to develop in you a heart of compassion for them. Ask God to give you a desire to reach out to these people with his love, both in word and action.

Anyone who isn't used to praying aloud should feel free to offer prayers in silence. Or, if you're new to prayer and you're feeling brave, try praying just one sentence: "God, please draw

_____ to yourself."

## STUDY NOTES

*Had compassion.* To feel sympathy or pity from the depth of one's gut. Compare James 5:11; Psalm 103:13. This kind of compassion moves one to action.

*Harassed.* Physically exhausted and troubled. "Distressed" (NASB) or stressed. Often when we are most tired, we are also emotionally spent.

*Helpless.* Literally, "thrown down." NASB translates this word as "downcast." The image is of a sheep that has slipped and fallen onto its back and is unable to turn over and stand up. The sheep exhausts itself in the struggle to stand. A downcast sheep can die if the shepherd doesn't find and rescue it.

*Harvest.* Jesus uses the picture of a harvest to describe the gathering of people into the kingdom of God. The crops are people ready to believe in Jesus. When we see people as they truly are, we feel Jesus' compassion for their plight and are motivated to go into the field (world) for harvest.

---

☐ *For Further Study* on this topic, read Luke 13:34; 23:28-43.

☐ *Weekly Memory Verse:* John 3:16

☐ *The Purpose-Driven Life Reading Plan:* Day 36

---

If you're using the DVD along
with this curriculum, please use
this space to take notes on the
teaching for this session.

# LOOKING BENEATH THE SURFACE

**D**enise and I thought all was well when we moved into a middle-class neighborhood. Our neighbors seemed like any other neighbors in an American suburb. But late one evening, a wife called us. She pleaded with us to rescue her husband. To all appearances he was a functioning father and employee, yet he had been addicted to crack for fifteen years. We were so saddened! He had always seemed "fine" to us.

After a dramatic rescue and extremely difficult rehabilitation, he finally welcomed the love and forgiveness of Jesus Christ. Now, several years later, his eyes and heart reveal the grace of Jesus and the hope of life-change for each of us.

Denise and I are no longer surprised to discover the addictions and the sin issues that fester in homes all around us. On the outside, all seems well. Taking a deeper look, however, we find that people desperately need the saving grace of Jesus Christ.

—Todd

## CONNECTING WITH GOD'S FAMILY                    10 min.

Some people seem to have no need for Jesus. They appear to be doing fine on their own. Others seem to be such a bundle of needs that we're reluctant to get involved. One important skill in sharing the gospel is the ability to see past someone's surface appearance to his or her heart, which holds real needs that Jesus is waiting to address. You may feel you lack this skill, but you *can* learn it. People's needs can be

- physical (food, shelter, a way to make a living, health, protection from physical harm).
- relational (respect, acceptance, receiving love, having one's love received by others, a way to count for good in the world, protection from emotional harm, relief from loneliness, freedom from political oppression).

- spiritual (a connection with God, an awareness of being part of something larger than oneself, clarity about what's important in life, forgiveness for wrongdoing, eternal life, peace).

This is just a partial list of needs; there are, of course, many others.

1. Recall a time when you were considering whether to put your faith in Jesus Christ. What were some of your unmet needs at the time?

How obvious do you think your needs were to people around you? Explain.

### GROWING TO BE LIKE CHRIST                                    20 min.

Jesus was brilliant at seeing past people's defenses and into their hearts. In this story, he zeroed in on the real needs of a Samaritan woman. See the study notes on page 30 for an explanation of the ethnic conflict between the Jews and the Samaritans.

*Now [Jesus] had to go through Samaria. ⁵So he came to a town in Samaria called Sychar, near the plot of ground Jacob had given to his son Joseph. ⁶Jacob's well was there, and Jesus, tired as he was from the journey, sat down by the well. It was about the sixth hour.*

*⁷When a Samaritan woman came to draw water, Jesus said to her, "Will you give me a drink?" ⁸(His disciples had gone into the town to buy food.)*

⁹The Samaritan woman said to him, "You are a Jew and I am a Samaritan woman. How can you ask me for a drink?" (For Jews do not associate with Samaritans.)

¹⁰Jesus answered her, "If you knew the gift of God and who it is that asks you for a drink, you would have asked him and he would have given you living water."

¹¹"Sir," the woman said, "you have nothing to draw with and the well is deep. Where can you get this living water? ¹²Are you greater than our father Jacob, who gave us the well and drank from it himself, as did also his sons and his flocks and herds?"

¹³Jesus answered, "Everyone who drinks this water will be thirsty again, ¹⁴but whoever drinks the water I give him will never thirst. Indeed, the water I give him will become in him a spring of water welling up to eternal life."

¹⁵The woman said to him, "Sir, give me this water so that I won't get thirsty and have to keep coming here to draw water."

¹⁶He told her, "Go, call your husband and come back."

¹⁷"I have no husband," she replied.

Jesus said to her, "You are right when you say you have no husband. ¹⁸The fact is, you have had five husbands, and the man you now have is not your husband. What you have just said is quite true."

¹⁹"Sir," the woman said, "I can see that you are a prophet. ²⁰Our fathers worshiped on this mountain, but you Jews claim that the place where we must worship is in Jerusalem."

²¹Jesus declared, "Believe me, woman, a time is coming when you will worship the Father neither on this mountain nor in Jerusalem. ²²You Samaritans worship what you do not know; we worship what we do know, for salvation is from the Jews. ²³Yet a time is coming and has now come when the true worshipers will worship the Father in spirit and truth, for they are the kind of worshipers the Father seeks. ²⁴God is spirit, and his worshipers must worship in spirit and in truth."

²⁵The woman said, "I know that Messiah" (called Christ) "is coming. When he comes, he will explain everything to us."

²⁶Then Jesus declared, "I who speak to you am he."

*27Just then his disciples returned and were surprised to find him talking with a woman. But no one asked, "What do you want?" or "Why are you talking with her?"*

*28Then, leaving her water jar, the woman went back to the town and said to the people, 29"Come, see a man who told me everything I ever did. Could this be the Christ?"*

—John 4:4–29

2. Jesus started a connection with this woman by pointing not at her need but at his own need (verses 4–9). What did Jesus say about his need?

Why do you think Jesus did this?

3. Reflect on the woman's response when Jesus did this. What do you think she was feeling and thinking?

4. Having gotten the woman's attention, Jesus pointed out her need (verses 10–15). What did she think she needed?

**5.** Jesus thought she needed "living water." What did he mean?

**6.** How did Jesus help her face her real need (verses 16–26)?

**7.** What do you think would have happened if Jesus had headed straight for her real need when he first spoke to her?

**8.** How did Jesus earn this woman's trust?

**9.** Think of someone in your life who doesn't believe in Jesus. What real needs do you see in this person?

**10.** Pause to pray for the people who come to your mind. Ask God to show you their real needs and guide you in responding to them wisely.

## SHARING YOUR LIFE MISSION EVERY DAY          30–40 min.

Most of us want to reach out to the people around us, but busyness and fear often distract us. It's helpful to give ourselves a structure that will support us in taking a step forward.

11. The Purpose-Driven Life Health Assessment on page 72 is a tool to help you identify areas where God might want to work in your life. Take a few minutes right now to rate yourself in the SHARING section of the assessment. You won't have to share your scores with the group.

12. Pair up with your partner from last week or someone in the group with whom you feel comfortable discussing your assessment. We recommend that men partner with men and women with women. Groups of three are also fine. Talk about these three questions:

    • **What's hot?** (In what ways are you doing well?)
    • **What's not?** (In which areas do you need the most growth?)
    • **What's next?** (What is one goal that you think God would like you to work on over the next thirty days? What will you do to reach that goal?)

    Here are examples of possible goals:

    ☐ I will pray daily for _____
      [an unchurched relative or friend].
    ☐ I will take time to show love to _____
      in a practical way.
    ☐ I will talk about faith in Jesus Christ with one
      unchurched person.
    ☐ I will maintain the group's Top Ten list. I will remind
      group members to pray for these persons each week, and
      I'll ask group members to share whether they've had a
      chance to reach out to them.
    ☐ I will start praying for and financially supporting a
      missionary.

Write your goal here:

The person you've paired up with can be your spiritual partner to support you in reaching your goal. In two of the next four group sessions you will briefly check in with your spiritual partner about your personal progress. You can also call or send an E-mail to each other between meetings. It's astonishing how a little prayer and encouragement strengthens us to share Christ's love!

If you've never taken the Purpose-Driven Life Health Assessment, consider rating yourself in the remaining four areas on your own this week.

 **SURRENDERING** YOUR LIFE FOR GOD'S PLEASURE   15–20 min.

13. Stay with your spiritual partner(s) for prayer. Take a few minutes to share any other prayer requests that haven't already come up in your discussion. Then pray for each other, especially for the strength to follow through on the goals you've set. If you're new to group prayer, it's okay to pray silently or to pray by using just one sentence: "God, please help _____ to _____."

As you leave, remember

• your goal for the next thirty days.
• to keep on with your daily devotions.
• to hide God's Word in your heart through your weekly Scripture memory verse.

## STUDY NOTES

Just as we do today, people in Jesus' time were quick to notice ethnic differences and divide the world into "us" and "them." They saw ethnic differences as reasons to look down on others. Jesus ignored those barriers to a degree unheard-of in his time. He simply saw people with needs.

*Samaritan woman.* Most Jews of Jesus' day looked down on Samaritans. Samaria was an ethnically mixed society with Jewish and pagan ancestry. Samaritan religion included Jewish and non-Jewish elements. Most Jews regarded Samaria as a "bad neighborhood" and avoided even traveling through it. Moreover, a good Jewish rabbi would never be seen talking to any woman, let alone a Samaritan woman, because women were seen as a corrupting influence. And this particular woman was an outcast even in her own community—that's why she was drawing water alone in the hottest part of the day instead of with the other women during the evening hours. As a rough analogy, you might picture a pastor or small group leader walking through the worst part of town and striking up a conversation with a prostitute.

*Living water.* Jesus promised to give the woman what she truly desired, namely, water that would never run out. She was thinking of her physical need. Jesus pointed to her spiritual need. Living water literally meant running as opposed to stagnant water. Jesus used the term metaphorically to refer to the Holy Spirit, who cleanses people from sin and satisfies their thirst for God (see John 7:37–39; Isaiah 12:3; 35:7; Zechariah 14:8).

*Five husbands.* The woman confronted her need for spiritual cleansing when Jesus pointed out her sin. We are often blind to the real problems that plague us. When we see them for what they are, we have a choice: We can decide to change, or we can reject the insight and go back to our self-delusion.

---

*For Further Study* on this topic, read Luke 19:1–10; Mark 10:17–22.

*Weekly Memory Verse:* Luke 19:10

*The Purpose-Driven Life Reading Plan:* Day 37

---

## Skill: Listening for Needs

With insight from the Holy Spirit, Jesus knew that the Samaritan woman had had five husbands. The Holy Spirit may not give you such dramatic insight about strangers, but he does desire to help you discern the felt needs and real needs of people around you. You can learn to notice the broken places in people's lives. Sensitive questions and practical acts, such as giving and receiving water, can speak powerfully to people about your respect and concern for them. Most people are as thirsty for respect and kindness as the Samaritan woman was.

Jesus modeled how to discern a person's real needs. As you listen to the needs someone expresses, you can simply ask a few caring questions that invite her to share more of her heart with you. By listening well, you can draw her out further.

The Five R's of Listening help keep a conversation going and create an atmosphere that draws someone out:

1. Rephrase what the person has shared with you.
2. Repeat his last sentence to encourage him to share more.
3. Return his comment with another question.
4. Respond with affirmation and gratitude for his willingness to share.
5. Renew your commitment to listen and pray for him.

If you're using the DVD along with this curriculum, please use this space to take notes on the teaching for this session.

# SESSION 3 — BUILDING BRIDGES THROUGH RELATIONSHIPS

Isn't it crazy to think that God can use BUNKO to build bridges to Jesus! My friend joined a BUNKO group to meet other moms and to get out of the house once a month. Her goal was purely social. As the group has grown, conversation has deepened. Dinner is often served before the game, and a specific question is answered by each mom sitting around the table. The questions have led to candid reflections on the meaning of life, marriage, career, and parenting. These evenings give my friend an environment in which to plant many seeds and invite many of the women to church. Even when conversation turns to gossip and gripes about daily life, my friend always asks the Lord to give her opportunities to bridge others to the incredible love of Jesus Christ.

—Denise

## CONNECTING WITH GOD'S FAMILY                              10 min.

Life these days seems to be packed to the brim! We can't imagine tacking on evangelism as an extra activity on top of work, family, church, and all the rest. But evangelism doesn't have to be an extra activity. Most of us come across unbelievers in the natural course of our lives—they are the parents of kids on our children's soccer teams, they work in our workplaces, they live across the street, they bag our groceries. Simply opening our eyes to the people we encounter gives us many opportunities to share God's love.

1. During a typical week, when and where do you interact with non-Christians?

## GROWING TO BE LIKE CHRIST

People don't care what we know until they know that we care. In most cases, relationships are crucial bridges we need to cross in order to win a hearing for the gospel.

Yet many Christians resist making friends with non-Christians. Sometimes the barrier is immoral behavior—can Christians befriend an unmarried couple living together, or does doing so amount to condoning sin? Sometimes the barrier is trust—can Christians trust people who don't share their deepest beliefs and values? Sometimes the barrier is different interests—do Christians want to spend time with people who don't enjoy church, Christian music, Christian books, Bible study, and so on? Sometimes the issue is temptation—can a Christian spend time with certain people and manage to avoid adopting their bad habits?

When Paul set out to take the gospel to unbelievers, he thought through these issues. Here's what he decided:

> Even though I am free of the demands and expectations of everyone, I have voluntarily become a servant to any and all in order to reach a wide range of people: [20]religious, nonreligious, [21]meticulous moralists, loose-living immoralists, [22]the defeated, the demoralized—whoever. I didn't take on their way of life. I kept my bearings in Christ—but I entered their world and tried to experience things from their point of view. I've become just about every sort of servant there is in my attempts to lead those I meet into a God-saved life. [23]I did all this because of the Message. I didn't just want to talk about it; I wanted to be in on it!
>
> —1 Corinthians 9:19-23 THE MESSAGE

**2.** Paul says, "I have voluntarily become a servant to any and all." What are some ways of being a servant to unbelievers?

3. What does it cost a Christian to become a servant to unbelievers? *Time ; understanding and patience.*

4. Why would a person choose to do this? *To build/improve a relationship. Also, to increase the chances for evangelizing.*

5. Paul says, "I didn't take on their way of life. I kept my bearings in Christ—but I entered their world and tried to experience things from their point of view." How would this stance help a person who is building friendships with unbelievers who are sexually immoral?

6. What do you think Paul would say to Christians who simply prefer to spend time with fellow Christians who share their values and interests?

**7.** What are your honest feelings about spending more time with unbelievers?

## SHARING YOUR LIFE MISSION EVERY DAY          20 min.

**8.** Is there anyone on your Top Ten list with whom you (perhaps along with other group members) could build a deeper relationship? How can you go about doing this? (For example, you might go running together, call and ask how they are *really* doing, or have them over for coffee.)

## SURRENDERING YOUR LIFE FOR GOD'S PLEASURE  15–30 min.

**9.** Sit next to your spiritual partner(s). Together do one or more of the following:

- Share what you learned from your devotional time this week.
- Recite your memory verse.
- Tell how you're doing with the goal you set for yourself.

**10.** How can the group pray for you this week? Be sure to pray for your Top Ten list.

## STUDY NOTES

*Voluntarily become a servant.* Or "slave" (NASB). Paul put other people's interests ahead of his own, not because he was forced to do so (he did it *voluntarily*) or because he bowed to pressure ("demands and expectations" didn't scare him). He didn't just do what made people happy in order to win their approval. He was able to set aside all of that and concern himself with doing good to others in their areas of genuine need. Groveling and people pleasing don't soften others' hearts for the gospel—but freely serving them does. In our world it's astonishing for one person to serve another without pressure or without strings attached. This is how we need to act toward unbelievers routinely.

*Entered their world and tried to experience things from their point of view.* The longer we've been believers, the further removed we often become from the world unbelievers live in. We may lose touch with their music, their political assumptions, their social events. We often see their world as immoral—as something that poses a danger to our own purity. But Paul challenges us to build our Christ-centered convictions while remaining engaged with the non-Christian world. It requires humility and strong character to spend time among gossips without gossiping, among cynics without becoming cynical, among the greedy without becoming greedy, among the sexually immoral without becoming sexually immoral. But this is exactly what Paul asks us to do.

---

☐ *For Further Study* on this topic, read Philippians 1:27–30; 2:14–16; 1 Thessalonians 2:5–12.

☐ *Weekly Memory Verse:* 2 Corinthians 5:20

☐ *The Purpose-Driven Life Reading Plan:* Day 38

---

If you're using the DVD along
with this curriculum, please use
this space to take notes on the
teaching for this session.

My husband, Greg, claims not to be good at sharing his faith. He will assert this with his dying breath. The irony is that he talks about Jesus Christ with non-Christians in the most natural way—more than anybody I know. He has one friend of many years who abandoned religion long ago, but whenever she teases him about "his Jesus," he teases her back until they're engaged in a serious discussion about faith. He tells her to her face that he knows she'll give in someday, and they both laugh. I have a relative with whom I have no idea how to have conversations about Christian faith, but Greg and he are great friends who seem to get into those conversations all the time. Greg will admit that he does seize every opportunity to fan into flame any spark of spiritual interest he sees in anybody, but he says that he's just being himself and not doing anything remarkable. "Anybody can do what I do," he insists. "Christ is just part of who I am, so of course I say so." And, of course, he's right. Anybody can do what he does. Even me. Even you.

—Karen

## CONNECTING WITH GOD'S FAMILY                     10 min.

1. Think of one person in your life who doesn't believe in Christ. Imagine starting a conversation about faith with that person. What thoughts or feelings go through your mind when you imagine that?

## GROWING TO BE LIKE CHRIST

The apostle Paul had a strategy for spreading the news about Jesus Christ throughout the Roman Empire. He would arrive in a city, convince a few key people whose hearts God had already prepared for the message, and train them and their households in the basics of the faith. Then he would move on, leaving the rest of the city in their hands. This handful of believers would then spread the news naturally through the network of relationships they already had. Outsiders would watch how Christ transformed the way these believers related to each other and to their neighbors. They would watch how these believers dealt with suffering. And they would start to ask questions. Paul tried to equip the fledgling believers to answer these questions in ways that would make sense to people who had no knowledge of the Bible.

Sharing our faith scares many Christians today. We fear we need to be Paul in order to be effective. But if we listen to the letters Paul wrote to small groups of young believers, we find that sharing our faith can be a natural part of our life together:

> Devote yourselves to prayer, being watchful and thankful.
> ³And pray for us, too, that God may open a door for our
> message, so that we may proclaim the mystery of Christ, for
> which I am in chains. ⁴Pray that I may proclaim it clearly, as
> I should. ⁵Be wise in the way you act toward outsiders; make
> the most of every opportunity. ⁶Let your conversation be always
> full of grace, seasoned with salt, so that you may know how to
> answer everyone.
> —Colossians 4:2–6

2. What role does Paul think prayer should play if we want to spread the news of Jesus Christ?

Why do you think prayer is so important?

3. Paul says that in our relationships with outsiders we should "make the most of every opportunity." What kinds of opportunities do you think he has in mind?

4. Paul also urges us to be wise in the way we act toward outsiders. Imagine yourself with a colleague from work, with a relative, or with your child's teacher. What actions would be wise if you want to be the kind of person who makes others curious about your faith?

What actions would be unwise?

5. Paul wants our ordinary conversations with outsiders to be "full of grace, seasoned with salt." How would you describe a grace-full conversation?

6. Knowing "how to answer everyone" is the part that scares many Christians. We think this means that we need to have the training of a pastor. But Paul was writing to ordinary people who had believed in Jesus Christ for just a few years. If a non-Christian asked you a question about your faith and you didn't know how to answer it, what would be some good ways to handle the situation?

7. How do you think an ordinary Christian can go about learning how to answer people's questions and comments about the Christian faith?

## SHARING YOUR LIFE MISSION EVERY DAY               30 min.

Building relationships with non-Christians leads to opportunities for words about our faith. At this point many of us get stuck. What do you say about Jesus when people respond to your actions and give you an opportunity to speak? One helpful tool is the ability to tell your personal story of faith in a way an outsider can relate to. Others may question God's words in the Bible, but they can never discredit what he has done and is doing in your life.

8. What aspects of your story would an unbeliever identify with? Read over the following four areas, and talk about what you could say about each one:

### *What my life was like before I met Jesus*

What circumstances or attitudes would an unbeliever identify with? What was most important to you? What substitute(s) for God did you use to find meaning in your life? (Substitutes include sports/fitness, success at work, marriage, children, sex, making money, drugs/alcohol, having fun, entertainment, popularity, hobbies, and so on.)[1]

### *How I realized I needed Jesus*

What significant steps led up to your conversion? What needs, hurts, or problems made you dissatisfied with the way you were living without God? (Choose a theme.) How did God get your attention? What motivated you?[2]

---

[1]If you've been a Christian since childhood, it may not be helpful for you to describe what you were like at, say, five years old. However, at some point in your life you've probably been tempted to lean on a substitute instead of on Jesus. Maybe you were tempted to find your self-worth in a perfect marriage and family, but you've learned to let your family be imperfect while you depend on Jesus Christ alone. Maybe your career began to draw your love away from Jesus, but now you've put your career in its proper subordinate place. Sinners trust Jesus partly because he admitted to being tempted in every way (Hebrews 4:15). If even Jesus was thoroughly tempted in ways sinners can identify with, the same is very likely true of you.

[2]If you've been a Christian since childhood, talk about a more recent temptation or a time of suffering when you needed Jesus.

### How I committed my life to Jesus

What specifically did you do to step across the line? Where did it happen? What did you say in your prayer? Be specific.[3]

### The difference this choice has made in my life

What benefits have you experienced or felt? What problems have been resolved? How has Jesus helped you change for the better? How has he helped your relationships? Give a current example.[4]

---

[3]If you've been a Christian since childhood, talk about what you did to turn to Jesus in that time of temptation or suffering. Be sure to include admitting your need for forgiveness, because this is something unbelievers rarely hear people admit.

[4]If you've been a Christian since childhood, talk about how God protected you, cared for you, and forgave you in your time of temptation or suffering. Also talk about how this experience continues to affect your life.

## SURRENDERING YOUR LIFE FOR GOD'S PLEASURE  15–30 min.

Paul says that prayer opens doors for opportunities to share our faith (Colossians 4:3). He also says that prayer can prepare us to be more effective in sharing with others (verse 4). Keep these thoughts in mind as you pray together.

9. Team up with another set of spiritual partners to form a prayer circle. Share prayer requests. Then pray for each other, especially to have opportunities this week to talk about your faith gracefully. Pray also for the people on your Top Ten list and for your own heart toward them. If you prefer to pray silently, you can simply say "amen" to let the others know you're finished.

## STUDY NOTES

*Watchful.* Literally, "keeping awake"—that is, spiritually alert.[5] (See also Matthew 26:41.) We are to remain prayerful and ever alert for opportunities to share our faith.

*Open a door for our message.* Literally, "a door of speaking." The phrase is used figuratively to describe the ripe opportunity to speak the gospel to another. Pray for God to prepare people to hear about and come to a better understanding of Jesus.

*Full of grace, seasoned with salt.* Our gracious words are like salt that gives flavor to food. Gracious words are considerate and attractive to the listener. Gracious words don't criticize. They aren't defensive but speak truthfully in a loving way.

---

*For Further Study* on this topic, read Philippians 1:27–30; 2:14–18; 1 Corinthians 4:1–2; 1 Peter 2:11–25.

*Weekly Memory Verse:* Colossians 4:5

*The Purpose-Driven Life Reading Plan:* Day 39

---

[5]Curtis Vaughan, *Galatians.* Volume 11 in *The Expositor's Bible Commentary*, Frank E. Gaebelein, General Editor (Grand Rapids: Zondervan, 1981), 221.

# NOTES

If you're using the DVD along with this curriculum, please use this space to take notes on the teaching for this session.

# EXPLAINING THE GOSPEL

Years ago I was on a crew that was shooting a training film about evangelism. Most of the actors were non-Christians. In one scene, an actor played a Christian who was explaining the gospel in the most churchy language imaginable. He was entirely convincing. Afterward, over lunch, he leaned across the table and asked me in all seriousness, "So, what is *propitiation* anyway?"

Probably no one will ever ask you what propitiation is. But if you're like many of us, the very thought of having to explain what you believe concisely and in ordinary language may make you sweat. Fear not! Help is on the way.

—Karen

## CONNECTING WITH GOD'S FAMILY                    10 min.

1. Try to define the word *propitiation*. If you have no idea, make something up!

The "real" definition is in the leader's notes. Give a round of applause to the person who came closest, and another round to the person who came up with the most fun guess.

## GROWING TO BE LIKE CHRIST                    30 min.

At what point do our lives for Jesus translate into words about Jesus? It's when we have earned the right to speak about him with others. Whether it's someone we've just met or a longtime friend, there comes a time when we speak of what faith in Jesus Christ is all about. The apostle Peter urges us to overcome our fears about that moment:

*Who is going to harm you if you are eager to do good? ¹⁴But even if you should suffer for what is right, you are blessed. "Do not fear what they fear; do not be frightened." ¹⁵But in your hearts set apart Christ as Lord. Always be prepared to give an answer to everyone who asks you to give the reason for the hope that you have. But do this with gentleness and respect, ¹⁶keeping a clear conscience, so that those who speak maliciously against your good behavior in Christ may be ashamed of their slander. ¹⁷It is better, if it is God's will, to suffer for doing good than for doing evil.*

—1 Peter 3:13–17

2. What reasons does Peter give for not being afraid to talk about Jesus with someone?

What do you think about these reasons?

3. Peter refers to the gospel as "the reason for the hope that you have" (verse 15). Read the definition of *hope* in the study notes. Do you experience that kind of hope? Explain your thoughts.

4. When we explain the gospel to someone, *how* should we go about it (verses 15–16)?

Why are gentleness and respect so important?

What exactly is the gospel we're sharing with people? Paul offers this summary:

*Now, brothers, I want to remind you of the gospel I preached to you, which you received and on which you have taken your stand. ²By this gospel you are saved, if you hold firmly to the word I preached to you. Otherwise, you have believed in vain.*

*³For what I received I passed on to you as of first importance: that Christ died for our sins according to the Scriptures, ⁴that he was buried, that he was raised on the third day according to the Scriptures, ⁵and that he appeared to Peter, and then to the Twelve. ⁶After that, he appeared to more than five hundred of the brothers at the same time, most of whom are still living, though some have fallen asleep. ⁷Then he appeared to James, then to all the apostles, ⁸and last of all he appeared to me also, as to one abnormally born.*

—1 Corinthians 15:1–8

**5.** The gospel focuses on what Jesus did. What are the important things Jesus did, according to this passage? Try to explain them in ordinary language that an unchurched person would understand.

**6.** Why is this good news and reason for hope?

 **SHARING** YOUR LIFE MISSION EVERY DAY          30 min.

The "Bridge Illustration" is an easy way to explain how to trust Jesus Christ for salvation. It shows what sin is, why sin separates us from God, how Jesus reconciles us to God, and what we need to do to accept Jesus' gift. When a person is ready to decide whether or not to follow Jesus, you can use the Bridge to clarify the issues in his or her mind.

7. Below is a box in which you can practice drawing the Bridge. After that you will find a script that gives you everything you need to explain the Bridge to someone else. Simply draw the picture step by step, and then ask the other person, "Where would you draw yourself in this illustration?"

*The Bridge to Life* © 2002 by The Navigators. Used by permission. Pocket-sized booklets with *The Bridge to Life* are available in packs of fifty from NavPress at www.navpress.com.

# THE **BRIDGE** TO LIFE

## Step 1 - God's Love and His plan

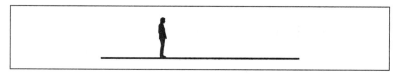

God created us in his own image to be his friend and to experience a full life assured of his love, abundant and eternal.

Jesus said, "I have come that they may have life, and have it to the full."

—John 10:10b

"We have peace with God through our Lord Jesus Christ."

—Romans 5:1

Since God planned for us to have peace and abundant life right now, why are most people not having this experience?

## Step 2 - Our Problem: Separation from God

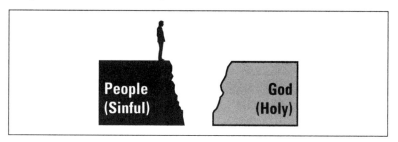

God created us in his own image to have abundant (meaningful) life. He did not make us robots to automatically love and obey him, but he gave us a will and a freedom of choice.

We chose to disobey God and go our own willful way. We still make this choice today. This results in separation from God.

"For all have sinned and fall short of the glory of God."

—Romans 3:23

On our own, there's no way we can attain the perfection needed to bridge the gap to God. Through the ages, individuals have tried many ways ... without success.

Good works won't do it ... or religion ... or money ... or morality ... or philosophy or ...

"There is a way that seems right to a man, but in the end it leads to death."
—Proverbs 14:12

## Step 3 - God's Remedy: The Cross

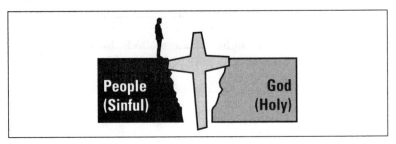

**Jesus Christ is the only answer to this problem. He died on the cross and rose from the grave, paying the penalty for our sin and bridging the gap between God and people.**

"For Christ died for sins once for all, the righteous for the unrighteous, to bring you to God."
—I Peter 3:18

"For there is one God and one mediator between God and men, the man Jesus Christ."
—I Timothy 2:5

"But God demonstrates his own love for us in this: While we were still sinners, Christ died for us."
—Romans 5:8

## Step 4 - Our Response

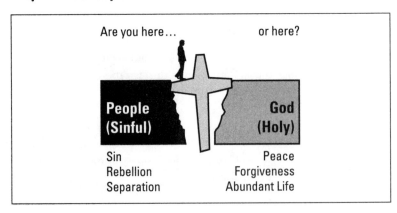

Believing means trust and commitment—acknowledging our sinfulness, trusting Christ's forgiveness, and letting him control our life. Eternal, abundant life is a gift for us to receive.

"For God so loved the world that he gave his one and only Son, that whoever believes in him shall not perish but have eternal life."

—John 3:16

"I tell you the truth, whoever **hears** my word and **believes** him who sent me has eternal life and will not be condemned; he has crossed over from death to life."

—John 5:24

Where would you draw yourself in this illustration?

What is keeping you from inviting Jesus into your life and crossing the Bridge to a relationship with God?

## How to Receive Christ

1. Admit your need (acknowledge, "I am a sinner").
2. Be willing to turn from your sins (repent).
3. Believe that Jesus Christ died for you on the cross and rose from the grave.
4. Through prayer, invite Jesus Christ to come in and rule your life through the Holy Spirit (receive him as Lord and Savior of your life).

> Dear Lord Jesus,
>
> I know that I am a sinner and need your forgiveness. I believe that you died for my sins. I want to turn from my sins. I now invite you to come into my heart and life. I want to trust and follow you as the Lord and Savior of my life. In Jesus' name. Amen.

**8.** Divide into groups of two or three people. Give each person a chance to practice sharing the Bridge illustration.

## SURRENDERING YOUR LIFE FOR GOD'S PLEASURE  15–30 min.

**9.** Sit next to your spiritual partner(s). Together do one or more of the following:

- Share what you learned from your devotional time this week.
- Recite your memory verse.
- Tell how you're doing with the goal you set for yourself.

**10.** The Lord's Supper, or Communion, is a wonderful way to celebrate Jesus' death and resurrection for you. It's a reminder of the gospel's core. Consider sharing Communion next week. Who is willing to lead it? Who will bring the elements?

*Instructions for sharing Communion in a small group are on page 78.*

**11.** Some of us feel nervous about inviting others to make a decision about Jesus Christ. What if we sit down to draw the Bridge and forget the verses? What if our friend doesn't respond well? As you pray for the needs of group members, include a prayer for courage—even boldness. Ask God to put in your life one person who is ready to make a decision to follow Jesus. Keep praying for the persons on your Top Ten list.

## STUDY NOTES

**An answer.** A verbal explanation of what we believe. The word literally means "defense," but we *shouldn't* be defensive. Our ego should not be at stake. Someone can reject our beliefs and not disrupt our confidence, because our confidence doesn't lie in what people think. Our explanation is made up of what the Bible says about our salvation and of our own personal story of salvation.

*Hope.* Hope is waiting for, groaning for, and fully expecting eventually to get something we want but don't yet have (Romans 8:22–25). In order to hope, we must intensely want something we don't have—and that's not always pleasant. Like pregnancy and birthing pain, hope includes both eager anticipation and agony. Christians place their hope in two things. First, we hope confidently that the Holy Spirit will continually help us become more loving, joyful, and brave persons in this life, no matter what happens to us. Second, we hope confidently that someday we will be welcomed into the kingdom of God in its fullness, where there will be feasting, celebration, joyous reunions, God's intimate presence, and an end to sorrow and pain (Isaiah 25:6–8; Revelation 21:1–5).

*Gospel.* Literally, "good news." If a doctor told you that your medical tests came back and you don't have cancer after all, *that* would be great news, wouldn't it? Even better news is that Jesus died for your sins and so enables you to live for eternity with God.

*Saved.* Rescued from danger or destruction. When we say that the gospel saves us, we mean that Jesus' death rescued us from the penalty for our sin. Sin is rebellion against God. The penalty for sin is eternal separation from God— a horrible fate because God is the source of all joy. Jesus rescued us from this separation.

*Died for our sins.* If you burned down someone's house, and the judge both went to jail in your place and paid for the house to be rebuilt, this would be something like what Jesus did on the cross. Your sins are like a crime and a debt you can't pay. The cost is more money than you make in a lifetime. For God to release you from the debt, someone else has to pay the debt for you. The debt can't simply be ignored, because someone has to pay to rebuild the house. Sin means you have been torching God's property all your life. Even pretty good people do far more damage than they like to admit. Jesus paid the price to restore what you have harmed and also to restore you to the person you were made to be.

---

☐ *For Further Study on this topic, read Proverbs 14:12; John 3:16– 21; 10:10; Romans 3:9–18, 21–26; 5:1–2, 6–8.*

☐ *Weekly Memory Verse:* 2 Peter 3:9

☐ *The Purpose-Driven Life Reading Plan:* Day 40

---

If you're using the DVD along with this curriculum, please use this space to take notes on the teaching for this session.

M ost of us ~~Anglos~~ Americans in the United States aren't raised with much cross-cultural experience. It's a stretch for us to visit the Arab grocery store across town, never mind participate in spreading the gospel in another country! Because we live two hours from Mexico, we have seized the chance to show our kids and ourselves that we really can have life together with other nations.

One year our family drove to Mexico with a church group to give Christmas presents to children at orphanages. We stopped for tacos just past the border and then traveled on to a few orphanages. There we played with the kids and told them that Jesus loved them and wanted to have a personal relationship with them. One little boy wanted his picture taken with our six-year-old son, Brandon. He showed Brandon where he slept and kept his stash of toys. That day Brandon learned that he could share Jesus' love with someone who didn't even speak his language, just by being himself. Life together became bigger than he'd ever guessed possible.

—Todd and Denise

## CONNECTING WITH GOD'S FAMILY                    10 min.

1. What has been the high point of this study for you?

2. What do you appreciate most about this group?
   *Willingness to share... understanding*
   *~ advice*

57

## GROWING TO BE LIKE CHRIST 30 min.

A person's last words before going away are often the thoughts closest to his or her heart. After Jesus rose from the dead, he spent forty days guiding his disciples. Then he ascended into heaven and was no longer bodily present on earth. What were his parting words that would encourage his followers for the task ahead?

> Then the eleven disciples went to Galilee, to the mountain where Jesus had told them to go. ¹⁷When they saw him, they worshiped him; but some doubted. ¹⁸Then Jesus came to them and said, "All authority in heaven and on earth has been given to me. ¹⁹Therefore go and make disciples of all nations, baptizing them in the name of the Father and of the Son and of the Holy Spirit, ²⁰and teaching them to obey everything I have commanded you. And surely I am with you always, to the very end of the age."
>
> —Matthew 28:16–20

3. What four things did Jesus tell his disciples to do?

4. Why do you think he chose these as his final words to his disciples?

5. What's your personal reaction to these words? (Do you feel urgency, inspiration, excitement, fear? Do you have mixed feelings?)

**6.** When Jesus talked about "everything I have commanded you" (verse 20), what commands do you think he had in mind? Give some examples.

**7.** In Jesus' day, teaching was not the transfer of information. It was hands-on training for doing something. You didn't find out if someone had learned Jesus' commands by giving them an essay test; you watched what they did. For example, Jesus said, "Go and make disciples of all nations." The test of whether we've learned to obey this command is our actual behavior toward people from other countries and cultures.

What contact with people from other cultures do you or could you have in a typical week? For example:

- Which students in your children's classes have families who come from other cultures?
- Who in your workplace comes from another culture?
- What contact do you have with anyone in other countries?
- When do you travel to other countries?
- How can you pay more attention to international news?
- Which overseas missionaries can you support?

**8.** What goes through your mind when you think about widening your circle of love to embrace people from other cultures and even other continents?

## SHARING YOUR LIFE MISSION EVERY DAY          20 min.

If you had to make disciples of all nations on your own, it would be overwhelming! But that's the point of life together—you have each other to rely on, and the Holy Spirit, too. In this final session, think about what you can do to team up with other group members to draw outsiders into life with Jesus Christ.

9. What step can you take as a group to continue to reach out to unbelievers? Here are some possibilities. Make a plan!

☐ Have a barbecue for group members and your non-Christian friends. Invite kids if you like. When you introduce one another, identify group members as "some people I meet with regularly to talk about how to live with joy and purpose." Some of your guests may be interested in joining your group—or even an offshoot of your group that would be geared to seekers.

☐ Instead of a barbecue, hold a women's coffee, a men's sports night, a holiday party, or some other social event.

☐ If you enjoy running, golfing, or some other hobby, invite a group member and a non-Christian friend to join you.

☐ Rent a movie that offers enough substance for a discussion about spiritual issues. Invite a couple of Christians and a couple of non-Christians to watch the movie and talk about it.

☐ Notice a neighbor's need. Does an elderly woman need leaves raked from her lawn? Join a couple of group members to do the job. Let her know you're in a group together that looks for ways to offer people the love of Jesus Christ.

☐ If you have contact (through work or school, for example) with someone from another culture, make a special point of including this person in your outreach plan.

☐ Support a missionary together. If your church doesn't already sponsor anyone, join together to identify a missions organization and an individual you can support.

☐ Write a letter to encourage a missionary you already support.

☐ Together sponsor a child for World Vision or Compassion International (or another child sponsorship agency).

☐ Pray for a country your group has chosen to "adopt."

10. What's next for your group? Turn to the Purpose-Driven Group Agreement on page 67. Do you want to agree to continue meeting together? If so, do you want to change anything in this agreement (times, dates, shared values, and so on)? Are there any things you'd like the group to do better as it moves forward? Take notes on this discussion.

11. How can the group pray for you this week?

12. Share Communion to celebrate this part of your journey together. In honoring Jesus and his death on the cross, Communion serves to keep what he has done for you in the front of your mind. It's an opportunity to reflect on why Jesus deserves to be worshiped and obeyed.

    *Instructions for sharing Communion in a small group are on page 78.*

## STUDY NOTES

*Make disciples.* This is the only true command in the passage. "Go," "baptizing," and "teaching" are all participles in the Greek; they describe how we are to make disciples. A disciple is both a learner and a follower of Jesus Christ. We are commanded to make disciples by going into the world and living among nonbelievers, leading them to Jesus, baptizing them in their new faith, and then teaching them to obey all that Jesus taught.

*I am with you always.* Jesus doesn't want us to let fear hold us back. He wants us to move forward in faith in him. He will give us the words to say (Matthew 10:26–33). He will be with us as we share our faith and make disciples.

---

☐ *For Further Study* on this topic, read Matthew 9:35–38; 10:1–42; Acts 1:8; 12:25; 13:4–5; 15:36, 41.

☐ *Weekly Memory Verse:* Matthew 28:19–20

---

If you're using the DVD along with this curriculum, please use this space to take notes on the teaching for this session.

# FREQUENTLY ASKED QUESTIONS

## Who may attend the group?

Anybody you feel would benefit from it. As you begin, we encourage each attender to invite at least one other friend to join. A good time to join is in the first or second week of a new study. Share the names of your friends with the group members so that they can be praying for you.

## How long will this group meet?

It's totally up to the group—once you come to the end of this six-week study. Most groups meet weekly for at least the first six weeks, but every other week can work as well. At the end of this study, each group member may decide if he or she wants to continue on for another six-week study. We encourage you to consider using the next study in this series. The series is designed to take you on a developmental journey to healthy, purpose-driven lives in thirty-six sessions. However, each guide stands on its own and may be taken in any order. You may take a break between studies if you wish.

## Who is the leader?

This booklet will walk you through every step for an effective group. In addition, your group may have selected one or more discussion leaders. We strongly recommend that you rotate the job of facilitating your discussions so that everyone's gifts can emerge and develop. You can share other responsibilities as well, such as bringing refreshments or keeping up with those who miss a meeting. There's no reason why one or two people need to do everything; in fact, sharing ownership of the group will help *everyone* grow. Finally, the Bible says that when two or more are gathered in Jesus' name (which you are), he is there in your midst. Ultimately, God is your leader each step of the way.

## Where do we find new members for our group?

This can be troubling, especially for new groups that have only a few people or for existing groups that lose a few people along the way. We encourage you to pray with your group and then brainstorm a list of people from work, church, your neighborhood, your children's school, family, the gym, and so forth. Then have each group member invite several of the people on their list. Another good strategy is to ask church leaders to make an announcement or to allow for a bulletin insert.

No matter how you find members, it's vital that you stay on the lookout for new people to join your group. All groups tend to go through some amount of healthy attrition—the result of moves, releasing new leaders, ministry opportunities, and so forth—and if the group gets too small, it could be at risk of shutting down. If you and your group stay open, you'll be amazed at the people God sends your way. The next person just might become a friend for life. You never know!

## How do we handle the child care needs in our group?

Very carefully. Seriously, this can be a sensitive issue. We suggest that you empower the group to openly brainstorm solutions. You may try something that works for some and not for others, so you must just keep playing with the dials. One common solution is to meet in the living room or dining room with the adults and to share the cost of a baby-sitter (or two) who can be with the kids in a different part of the house. Another popular option is to use one home for the kids and a second home (close by or a phone call away) for the adults. Finally, you could rotate the responsibility of providing a lesson of some sort for the kids. This last idea can be an incredible blessing to you and the kids. We've done it, and it's worked great! Again, the best approach is to encourage the group to dialogue openly about both the problem and the solution.

# PURPOSE-DRIVEN GROUP AGREEMENT

APPENDIX

It's a good idea for every group to put words to their shared values, expectations, and commitments. A written agreement will help you avoid unspoken agendas and disappointed expectations. You'll discuss your agreement in session 1, and then you'll revisit it in session 6 to decide whether you want to modify anything as you move forward as a group. (Alternatively, you may agree to end your group in session 6.) Feel free to modify anything that doesn't work for your group.

If the idea of having a written agreement is unfamiliar to your group, we encourage you to give it a try. A clear agreement is invaluable for resolving conflict constructively and for setting your group on a path to health.

## We agree to the following values:

| | |
|---|---|
| **Clear Purpose** | To grow healthy spiritual lives by building a healthy small group community. In addition, we _____ _____ _____ _____ _____ |
| **Group Attendance** | To give priority to the group meeting (call if I will be late or absent) |
| **Safe Environment** | To help create a safe place where people can be heard and feel loved (please, no quick answers, snap judgments, or simple fixes) |
| **Confidentiality** | To keep anything that is shared strictly confidential and within the group |
| **Spiritual Health** | To give group members permission to help me live a healthy spiritual life that is pleasing to God (see the health assessment and health plan) |

| | |
|---|---|
| **Inviting People** | To keep an open chair in our group and share Jesus' dream of finding a shepherd for every sheep by inviting newcomers |
| **Shared Ownership** | To remember that every member is a minister and to encourage each attender to share a small group role or serve on one of the purpose teams (page 70) |
| **Rotating Leaders** | To encourage someone new to facilitate the group each week and to rotate homes and refreshments as well (see Small Group Calendar) |
| **Spiritual Partners** | To pair up with one other group member whom I can support more diligently and help to grow spiritually (my spiritual partner is _____) |

## We agree to the following expectations:

• Refreshments/Mealtimes _____

• Child care _____

• When we will meet (day of week) _____

• Where we will meet (place) _____

• We will begin at (time)_____ and end at _____

• We will do our best to have some or all of us attend a worship service together. Our primary worship service time will be _____

• Review date of this agreement: _____

## We agree to the following commitment:

Father, to the best of my ability, in light of what I know to be true, I commit the next season of my life to CONNECTING with your family, GROWING to be more like Christ, DEVELOPING my shape for ministry, SHARING my life mission every day, and SURRENDERING my life for your pleasure.

| | | |
|---|---|---|
| _____ | _____ | _____ |
| Name | Date | Spiritual Partner (witness) |

# SMALL GROUP CALENDAR

Healthy purpose-driven groups share responsibilities and group ownership. This usually doesn't happen overnight but progressively over time. Sharing responsibilities and ownership ensures that no one person carries the group alone. The calendar below can help you in this area. You can also add a social event, mission project, birthdays, or days off to your calendar. This should be completed after your first or second meeting. Planning ahead will facilitate better attendance and greater involvement from others.

| Date | Lesson | Location | Dessert/Meal | Facilitator |
|------|--------|----------|--------------|-------------|
| Monday, January 15 | 1 | Steve and Laura's | Joe | Bill |
| | | | | |
| | | | | |
| | | | | |
| | | | | |
| | | | | |
| | | | | |
| | | | | |
| | | | | |
| | | | | |

# PURPOSE
# TEAM ROLES

The Bible makes clear that every member, not just the small group leader, is a minister in the body of Christ. In a purpose-driven small group (just like in a purpose-driven church), every member plays a role on the team. Review the team roles and responsibilities below and have each member volunteer for a role, or have the group suggest a role for each member. It's best to have one or two people on each team, so you have each purpose covered. Serving in even a small capacity will not only help your leader grow but will also make the group more fun for everyone. Don't hold back. Join a team!

The opportunities below are broken down by the five purposes and then by a *crawl* (beginning group role), *walk* (intermediate group role), or *run* (advanced group role). Try to cover the crawl and walk phases if you can.

| Purpose Team Roles | Purpose Team Members |
|---|---|
| **Fellowship Team**  (**CONNECTING** with God's Family) | |
| Crawl:  Host social events or group activities | _____ |
| Walk:  Serve as a small group inviter | _____ |
| Run:  Lead the CONNECTING time each week | _____ |
| **Discipleship Team**  (**GROWING** to Be Like Christ) | |
| Crawl:  Ensure that each member has a simple plan and a partner for personal devotions | _____ |
| Walk:  Disciple a few younger group members | _____ |
| Run:  Facilitate the Purpose-Driven Life Health Assessment and Purpose-Driven Life Health Plan processes | _____ |

### Ministry Team  (**DEVELOPING** Your Shape for Ministry)

Crawl: Ensure that each member finds a group role   _____
or a purpose team responsibility

Walk: Plan a ministry project for the group in the   _____
church or community

Run: Help each member discover and develop   _____
a SHAPE-based ministry in the church

### Evangelism (Missions) Team  (**SHARING** Your Life Mission Every Day)

Crawl: Coordinate the group prayer and praise list   _____
of non-Christian friends and family members

Walk: Pray for group mission opportunities and   _____
plan a group cross-cultural adventure

Run: Plan as a group to attend a holiday service,   _____
host a neighborhood party, or create a seeker
event for your non-Christian friends

### Worship Team  (**SURRENDERING** Your Life for God's Pleasure)

Crawl: Maintain the weekly group prayer and praise   _____
list or journal

Walk: Lead a brief worship time in your group   _____
(CD/video/a cappella)

Run: Plan a Communion time, prayer walk, foot   _____
washing, or an outdoor worship experience

# PURPOSE-DRIVEN LIFE HEALTH ASSESSMENT

| | Just Beginning | Getting Going | Well Developed |
|---|---|---|---|

## CONNECTING WITH GOD'S FAMILY

I am deepening my understanding of and friendship with God in community with others — 1 2 3 4 5

I am growing in my ability both to share and to show my love to others — 1 2 3 4 5

I am willing to share my real needs for prayer and support from others — 1 2 3 4 5

I am resolving conflict constructively and am willing to forgive others — 1 2 3 4 5

CONNECTING Total _____

## GROWING TO BE LIKE CHRIST

I have a growing relationship with God through regular time in the Bible and in prayer (spiritual habits) — 1 2 3 4 5

I am experiencing more of the characteristics of Jesus Christ (love, joy, peace, patience, kindness, self-control, etc.) in my life — 1 2 3 4 5

I am avoiding addictive behaviors (food, television, busyness, and the like) to meet my needs — 1 2 3 4 5

I am spending time with a Christian friend (spiritual partner) who celebrates and challenges my spiritual growth — 1 2 3 4 5

GROWING Total _____

## DEVELOPING YOUR SHAPE TO SERVE OTHERS

I have discovered and am further developing my unique God-given shape for ministry — 1 2 3 4 5

I am regularly praying for God to show me opportunities to serve him and others — 1 2 3 4 5

I am serving in a regular (once a month or more) ministry in the church or community — 1 2 3 4 5

I am a team player in my small group by sharing some group role or responsibility — 1 2 3 4 5

DEVELOPING Total_____

### **SHARING** YOUR LIFE MISSION EVERY DAY

I am cultivating relationships with non-Christians and praying
for God to give me natural opportunities to share his love    1 2 3 4 5

I am investing my time in another person or group who needs
to know Christ personally    1 2 3 4 5

I am regularly inviting unchurched or unconnected friends to
my church or small group    1 2 3 4 5

I am praying and learning about where God can use me and
our group cross-culturally for missions    1 2 3 4 5

SHARING Total _____

### **SURRENDERING** YOUR LIFE FOR GOD'S PLEASURE

I am experiencing more of the presence and power of God in
my everyday life    1 2 3 4 5

I am faithfully attending my small group and weekend services
to worship God    1 2 3 4 5

I am seeking to please God by surrendering every area of my life
(health, decisions, finances, relationships, future, etc.) to him    1 2 3 4 5

I am accepting the things I cannot change and becoming
increasingly grateful for the life I've been given    1 2 3 4 5

SURRENDERING Total_____

Total your scores for each purpose, and place them on the chart below. Reassess
your progress at the end of thirty days. Be sure to select your spiritual partner and
the one area in which you'd like to make progress over the next thirty days.

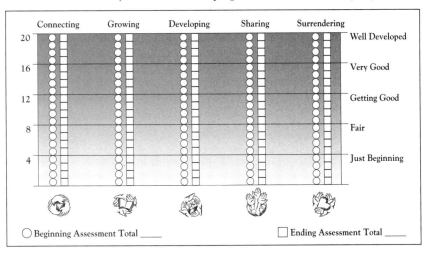

73

# PURPOSE-DRIVEN LIFE HEALTH PLAN

My Name _____ Date _____

My Spiritual Partner _____ Date _____

## Possibilities

## Plan
(make one goal for each area)

**CONNECTING** WITH GOD'S FAMILY
*Hebrews 10:24–25; Ephesians 2:19*
How can I deepen my relationships with others?

- Attend my group more faithfully

- Schedule lunch with a group member

- Begin praying for a spiritual mentor

WHO is/are my shepherd(s)?

NAME: _____

**GROWING** TO BE LIKE CHRIST
*Colossians 1:28; Ephesians 4:15*
How can I grow to be like Christ?

- Commit to personal time with God three days a week

- Ask a friend for devotional accountability

- Begin journaling my prayers

WHAT is my Spiritual Health Plan?

RENEWAL DATE: _____

### DEVELOPING YOUR SHAPE TO SERVE OTHERS
*Ephesians 4:11–13; 1 Corinthians 12:7; 1 Peter 3:10*
How can I develop my shape for ministry?

- Begin praying for a personal ministry

- Attend a gift discovery class

- Serve together at a church event or in the community

WHERE am I serving others?

MINISTRY: _____

### SHARING YOUR LIFE MISSION EVERY DAY
*Matthew 28:18–20; Acts 20:24*
How can I share my faith every day?

- Start meeting for lunch with a seeker friend

- Invite a non-Christian relative to church

- Pray for and support an overseas missionary

WHEN am I sharing my life mission?

TIME: _____

### SURRENDERING YOUR LIFE FOR GOD'S PLEASURE
How can I surrender my life for God's pleasure?

- Submit one area to God

- Be honest about my struggle and hurt

- Buy a music CD for worship in my car and in the group

HOW am I surrendering my life today?

AREA: _____

| | Progress (renew and revise) | Progress (renew and revise) | Progress (renew and revise) |
|---|---|---|---|
| | 30 days/Date _____ <br> ☐ ☐ ☐ ☐ <br> Weekly check-in with my spiritual partner or group | 60-90 days/Date _____ <br> ☐ ☐ ☐ ☐ <br> Weekly check-in with my spiritual partner or group | 120+ days/Date _____ <br> ☐ ☐ ☐ ☐ <br> Weekly check-in with my spiritual partner or group |
| CONNECTING | | | |
| GROWING | | | |
| DEVELOPING | | | |
| SHARING | | | |
| SURRENDERING | | | |

# SPIRITUAL PARTNERS'
# CHECK-IN PAGE

My Name _____   Spiritual Partner's Name _____

|        | Our Plans | Our Progress |
|--------|-----------|--------------|
| Week 1 |           |              |
| Week 2 |           |              |
| Week 3 |           |              |
| Week 4 |           |              |
| Week 5 |           |              |
| Week 6 |           |              |

Briefly check in each week and write down your personal plans and progress for the next week (or even for the next few weeks). This could be done (before or after the meeting) on the phone, through an E-mail message, or even in person from time to time.

# SERVING COMMUNION

Churches vary in their treatment of Communion (the Lord's Supper). Here is one simple form by which a small group can share this experience. You can adapt this form as necessary, depending on your church's beliefs.

## Steps in Serving Communion

1. Out of the context of your own experience, say something brief about God's love, forgiveness, grace, mercy, commitment, tenderheartedness, or faithfulness. Connect your words with the personal stories of the group. For example, "These past few weeks I've experienced God's mercy in the way he untangled the situation with my son. And I've seen God show mercy to others of us here too, especially to Jean and Roger." If you prefer, you can write down ahead of time what you want to say.

2. Read 1 Corinthians 11:23–26:

   *The Lord Jesus, on the night he was betrayed, took bread, [24]and when he had given thanks, he broke it and said, "This is my body, which is for you; do this in remembrance of me." [25]In the same way, after supper he took the cup, saying, "This cup is the new covenant in my blood; do this, whenever you drink it, in remembrance of me." [26]For whenever you eat this bread and drink this cup, you proclaim the Lord's death until he comes.*

3. Pray silently and pass the bread around the circle. While the bread is being passed, you may want to reflect quietly, sing a simple praise song, or listen to a worship tape.

4. When everyone has received the bread, remind them that this represents Jesus' broken body on their behalf. Simply state, "Jesus said, 'Do this in remembrance of me.' Let us eat together," and eat the bread as a group.

5. Pray silently and serve the cup. You may pass a small tray, serve people individually, or have them pick up a cup from the table.

6. When everyone has been served, remind them that the cup represents Jesus' blood shed for them. Simply state, "The cup of the new covenant is Jesus Christ's blood shed for you. Jesus said, 'Do this in remembrance of me.' Let us drink together." Then drink the juice as a group.

7. Conclude by singing a simple song, listening to a praise song, or having a time of prayer in thanks to God.

## Practical Tips in Serving Communion

1. Prepare the elements simply, sacredly, and symbolically.

2. Be sensitive to timing in your meeting.

3. Break up pieces of cracker or soft bread on a small plate or tray. *Don't* use large servings of bread or grape juice. We encourage you to use grape juice, not wine, because wine is a cause of stumbling for some people.

4. Have all of the elements prepared beforehand, and just bring them into the room or to the table when you are ready.

---

☐ **For Further Study**
*Other Communion passages: Matthew 26:26–29; Mark 14:22–25; Luke 22:14–20; 1 Corinthians 10:16–21; 11:17–34*

---

# APPENDIX

# MEMORY VERSES

One of the most effective ways to instill biblical truth deep into our lives is to memorize key Scriptures. For many, memorization is a new concept—or perhaps one we found difficult in the past. We encourage you to stretch yourself and try to memorize these six verses.

A good way to memorize a verse is to copy it on a sheet of paper five times. Most people learn something by heart when they do this. It's also helpful to post the verse someplace where you will see it several times a day.

## WEEK ONE

"For God so loved the world that he gave his one and only Son, that whoever believes in him shall not perish but have eternal life."

John 3:16

## WEEK TWO

"For the Son of Man came to seek and to save what was lost."

Luke 19:10

## WEEK THREE

"We are therefore Christ's ambassadors, as though God were making his appeal through us. We implore you on Christ's behalf: Be reconciled to God."

2 Corinthians 5:20

## WEEK FOUR

"Be wise in the way you act toward outsiders; make the most of every opportunity."

Colossians 4:5

## WEEK FIVE

"The Lord is not slow in keeping his promise, as some understand slowness. He is patient with you, not wanting anyone to perish, but everyone to come to repentance."

2 Peter 3:9

## WEEK SIX

"Therefore go and make disciples of all nations, baptizing them in the name of the Father and of the Son and of the Holy Spirit, and teaching them to obey everything I have commanded you. And surely I am with you always, to the very end of the age."

Matthew 28:19–20

# DAILY DEVOTIONAL READINGS

We've experienced so much life change as a result of reading the Bible daily. Hundreds of people have gone through DOING LIFE TOGETHER, and they tell us that the number-one contributor to their growth was the deeper walk with God that came as a result of the daily devotions. We strongly encourage you to have everyone set a realistic goal for the six weeks. Pair people into same-gender spiritual (accountability) partners. This will improve your results tenfold. Then we encourage everyone to take a few minutes each day to **READ** the verse for the day, **REFLECT** on what God is saying to you through the verse, and **RESPOND** to God in prayer in a personal journal. Each of these verses was selected to align with the week's study. After you complete the reading, simply put a check mark in the box next to the verse. Enjoy the journey!

## WEEK ONE
- ☐ Luke 4:38–41
- ☐ Luke 8:40–56
- ☐ John 8:1–11
- ☐ Luke 15:1–10
- ☐ Luke 15:11–32

## WEEK TWO
- ☐ Luke 19:1–10
- ☐ Matthew 9:9–12
- ☐ Acts 9:10–19
- ☐ Acts 10:34–35
- ☐ Mark 10:17–25

## WEEK THREE
- ☐ 1 Corinthians 3:6–8
- ☐ 2 Corinthians 4:1–6
- ☐ 2 Corinthians 4:7–12
- ☐ John 4:35–38
- ☐ Romans 10:13–15

## WEEK FOUR
- ☐ John 8:12
- ☐ John 17:15–19
- ☐ John 17:20–23
- ☐ Acts 20:24
- ☐ John 13:35

## WEEK FIVE
- ☐ John 10:10
- ☐ Romans 3:23
- ☐ 1 Timothy 2:5
- ☐ Ephesians 2:8–9
- ☐ John 1:12

## WEEK SIX
- ☐ Acts 1:8
- ☐ Acts 2:32–39
- ☐ Acts 17:24–28
- ☐ 1 John 4:7–12
- ☐ 1 John 4:13–18

# PRAYER AND
# PRAISE REPORT

Briefly share your prayer requests with the large group, making notations below. Then gather in small groups of two, three, or four to pray for each need.

|  | Prayer Request | Praise Report |
|---|---|---|
| Week 1 |  |  |
| Week 2 |  |  |
| Week 3 |  |  |

| | Prayer Request | Praise Report |
|---|---|---|
| Week 4 | | |
| Week 5 | | |
| Week 6 | | |

Today's Passage: _____

## Reflections from my HEART:

I **H**onor who you are. (Praise God for something.)

I **E**xpress who I'm not. (Confess any known sin.)

I **A**ffirm who I am in you. (How does God see you?)

I **R**equest your will for me. (Ask God for something.)

I **T**hank you for what you've done. (Thank him for something.)

## Today's Action Step:

# LEADERSHIP TRAINING

## Small Group Leadership 101 (Top Ten Ideas for New Facilitators)

Congratulations! You have responded to the call to help shepherd Jesus' flock. There are few other tasks in the family of God that surpass the contribution you will be making. As you prepare to lead—whether it is one session or the entire series—here are a few thoughts to keep in mind. We encourage you to read these and review them with each new discussion leader before he or she leads.

1. **Remember that you are not alone.** God knows everything about you, and he knew that you would be asked to lead your group. Even though you may not feel ready to lead, this is common for all good leaders. Moses, Solomon, Jeremiah, or Timothy—they *all* were reluctant to lead. God promises, "Never will I leave you; never will I forsake you" (Hebrews 13:5). Whether you are leading for one evening, for several weeks, or for a lifetime, you will be blessed as you serve.

2. **Don't try to do it alone.** Pray right now for God to help you build a healthy leadership team. If you can enlist a coleader to help you lead the group, you will find your experience to be much richer. This is your chance to involve as many people as you can in building a healthy group. All you have to do is call and ask people to help—you'll be surprised at the response.

3. **Just be yourself.** If you won't be you, who will? God wants to use your unique gifts and temperament. Don't try to do things exactly like another leader; do them in a way that fits you! Just admit it when you don't have an answer and apologize when you make a mistake. Your group will love you for it!—and you'll sleep better at night.

4. **Prepare for your meeting ahead of time.** Review the session and the leader's notes, and write down your responses to each question. Pay special attention to exercises that ask group members to do something other than engage in discussion. These exercises will help your group *live* what the Bible teaches, not just talk about it. Be sure you understand how an exercise works, and bring any necessary supplies (such as paper or pens) to your meeting. If the exercise employs one of the items in the appendix (such as the Purpose-Driven Life Health Assessment), be sure to look over that item so

you'll know how it works. Finally, review "Read Me First" on pages 11–14 so you'll remember the purpose of each section in the study.

5. **Pray for your group members by name.** Before you begin your session, go around the room in your mind and pray for each member by name. You may want to review the prayer list at least once a week. Ask God to use your time together to touch the heart of every person uniquely. Expect God to lead you to whomever he wants you to encourage or challenge in a special way. If you listen, God will surely lead!

6. **When you ask a question, be patient.** Someone will eventually respond. Sometimes people need a moment or two of silence to think about the question, and if silence doesn't bother you, it won't bother anyone else. After someone responds, affirm the response with a simple "thanks" or "good job." Then ask, "How about somebody else?" or "Would someone who hasn't shared like to add anything?" Be sensitive to new people or reluctant members who aren't ready to say, pray, or do anything. If you give them a safe setting, they will blossom over time.

7. **Provide transitions between questions.** When guiding the discussion, always read aloud the transitional paragraphs and the questions. Ask the group if anyone would like to read the paragraph or Bible passage. Don't call on anyone, but ask for a volunteer, and then be patient until someone begins. Be sure to thank the person who reads aloud.

8. **Break up into small groups each week, or they won't stay.** If your group has more than seven people, we strongly encourage you to have the group gather in discussion circles of three or four people during the GROWING or SURRENDERING sections of the study. With a greater opportunity to talk in a small circle, people will connect more with the study, apply more quickly what they're learning, and ultimately get more out of it. A small circle also encourages a quiet person to participate and tends to minimize the effects of a more vocal or dominant member. And it can help people feel more loved in your group. When you gather again at the end of the section, you can have one person summarize the highlights from each circle.

Small circles are also helpful during prayer time. People who are unaccustomed to praying aloud will feel more comfortable trying it with just two or three others. Also, prayer requests won't take as much time, so circles will have more time to actually pray. When you gather back with the whole group, you can have one person from each circle briefly update everyone on the prayer requests. People are more willing to pray in small circles if they know that the whole group will hear all the prayer requests.

9. **Rotate facilitators weekly.** At the end of each meeting, ask the group who should lead the following week. Let the group help select your weekly facilitator. You may be perfectly capable of leading each time, but you will help others grow in their faith and gifts if you give them opportunities to lead. You can use the Small Group Calendar on page 69 to fill in the names of all six meeting leaders at once if you prefer.

10. **One final challenge (for new or first-time leaders): Before your first opportunity to lead, look up each of the five passages listed below.** Read each one as a devotional exercise to help prepare yourself with a shepherd's heart. Trust us on this one. If you do this, you will be more than ready for your first meeting.

- [ ] Matthew 9:36
- [ ] 1 Peter 5:2-4
- [ ] Psalm 23
- [ ] Ezekiel 34:11–16
- [ ] 1 Thessalonians 2:7–8, 11–12

## Small Group Leadership Lifters (Weekly Leadership Tips)

*And David shepherded them with integrity of heart;*
*with skillful hands he led them.*

Psalm 78:73

David provides a model of a leader who has a heart for God, a desire to shepherd God's people, and a willingness to develop the skills of a leader. The following is a series of practical tips for new and existing small group leaders. These principles and practices have proved to cultivate healthy, balanced groups in over a thousand examples.

### 1. Don't Leave Home without It: A Leader's Prayer

"The prayer of a righteous man [or woman] is powerful and effective" (James 5:16). From the very beginning of this study, why not commit to a simple prayer of renewal in your heart and in the hearts of your members? Take a moment right now and write a simple prayer as you begin:

Father, help me _____

_____

_____

### 2. Pay It Now or Pay It Later: Group Conflict

Most leaders and groups avoid conflict, but healthy groups are willing to do what it takes to learn and grow through conflict. Much group conflict can be avoided if the leader lets the group openly discuss and decide its direction, using the Purpose-Driven Group Agreement. Healthy groups are alive. Conflict is a sign of maturity, not mistakes. Sometimes you may need to get outside counsel, but don't be afraid. See conflict as an opportunity to grow, and always confront it so it doesn't create a cancer that can kill the group over time (Matthew 18:15–20).

### 3. Lead from Weakness

The apostle Paul said that God's power was made perfect in Paul's weakness (2 Corinthians 12:9). This is clearly the opposite of what most leaders think, but it provides the most significant model of humility, authority, and spiritual power. It was Jesus' way at the cross. So share your struggles along with your successes, confess your sins to one another along with your celebrations, and ask for prayer for yourself along with praying for others. God will be pleased, and your group will grow deeper. If you humble yourself under God's mighty hand, he will exalt you at the proper time (Matthew 23:12).

### 4. What Makes Jesus Cry: A Leader's Focus

In Matthew 9:35–38, Jesus looked at the crowds following him and saw them as sheep without a shepherd. He was moved with compassion, because they were "distressed and downcast" (NASB); the NIV says they were "harassed and helpless." The Greek text implies that he was moved to the point of tears.

Never forget that you were once one of those sheep yourself. We urge you to keep yourself and your group focused not just inwardly to each other but also outwardly to people beyond your group. Jesus said, "Follow me ... and I will make you fishers of men" (Matthew 4:19). We assume that you and your group are following him. So how is your fishing going? As leader, you can ignite in your group Jesus' compassion for outsiders. For his sake, keep the fire burning!

### 5. Prayer Triplets

Prayer triplets can provide a rich blessing to you and many others. At the beginning or end of your group meeting, you can gather people into prayer triplets to share and pray about three non-Christian friends. This single strategy will increase your group's evangelistic effectiveness considerably. Be sure to get an update on the plans and progress from each of the circles. You need only ten minutes at every other meeting—but do this at least once a month. At first, some of your members may feel overwhelmed at the thought of praying for non-Christians. We've been there! But you can be confident that over time they will be renewed in their heart for lost people and experience the blessing of giving birth to triplets.

### 6. Race against the Clock

When your group grows in size or your members begin to feel more comfortable talking, you will inevitably feel as though you're racing against the clock. You may know the feeling very well. The good news is that there are several simple things that can help your group stick to your agreed schedule:

- The time crunch is actually a sign of relational and spiritual health, so pat yourselves on the back.
- Check in with the group to problem-solve, because they feel the tension as well.

- You could begin your meeting a little early or ask for a later ending time.
- If you split up weekly into circles of three to four people for discussion, you will double the amount of time any one person can share.
- Appoint a timekeeper to keep the group on schedule.
- Remind everyone to give brief answers.
- Be selective in the number of questions you try to discuss.
- Finally, planning the time breaks in your booklet before the group meeting begins can really keep you on track.

## 7. All for One and One for All: Building a Leadership Team

The statement "Together Everybody Accomplishes More" (TEAM) is especially true in small groups. The Bible clearly teaches that every member is a minister. Be sure to empower the group to share weekly facilitation, as well as other responsibilities, and seek to move every player onto a team over time. Don't wait for people to ask, because it just won't happen. From the outset of your group, try to get everybody involved. The best way to get people in the game is to have the group suggest who would serve best on what team and in what role. See Purpose Team Roles on pages 70–71 for several practical suggestions. You could also talk to people individually or ask for volunteers in the group, but don't miss this opportunity to develop every group member and build a healthy and balanced group over time.

## 8. Purpose-Driven Groups Produce Purpose-Driven Lives: A Leader's Goal

As you undertake this new curriculum, especially if this is your first time as a leader, make sure you begin with the end in mind. You may have heard the phrase, "If you aim at nothing, you'll hit it every time." It's vital for your group members to review their spiritual health by using the Purpose-Driven Life Health Assessment and Purpose-Driven Life Health Plan (pages 72–76). You'll do part of the health assessment in your group in session 2 and share your results with spiritual partners for support and accountability. Each member will also set one goal for thirty days. The goal will be tied to the purpose you are studying in this particular guide. We strongly encourage you to go even further and do the entire health assessment together. Then during another group session (or on their own), members can set a goal for each of the other four purposes.

Pairing up with spiritual partners will offer invaluable support for that area of personal growth. Encourage partners to pray for one another in the area of their goals. Have partners gather at least three times during the series to share their progress and plans. This will give you and the group the best results. In order for people to follow through with their goals, you'll need to lead with vision and modeling. Share your goals with the group, and update them on how the steps you're taking have been affecting your spiritual life. If you share your progress and plans, others will follow in your footsteps.

## 9. Discover the Power of Pairs

The best resolutions get swept aside by busyness and forgetfulness, which is why it's important for group members to have support as they pursue a spiritual goal. Have them pair up with spiritual partners in session 2, or encourage them to seek out a Christian coworker or personal mentor. You can promise that they'll never be the same if they simply commit to supporting each other with prayer and encouragement on a weekly basis.

It's best to start with one goal in an area of greatest need. Most of the time the area will be either evangelism or consistent time with the Father in prayer and in Scripture reading. Cultivating time with God is the place to start; if group members are already doing this, they can move on to a second and third area of growth.

You just need a few victories in the beginning. Have spiritual partners check in together at the beginning or end of each group meeting. Ask them to support those check-ins with phone calls, coffee times, and E-mail messages during the week. Trust us on this one—you will see people grow like never before.

## 10. Don't Lose Heart: A Leader's Vision

You are a strategic player in the heavenly realm. Helping a few others grow in Christ could put you squarely in the sights of Satan himself. First Corinthians 15:58 (NASB) says, "Be steadfast, immovable, always abounding in the work of the Lord." Leading a group is not always going to be easy. Here are the keys to longevity and lasting joy as a leader:

- Be sure to refuel your soul as you give of yourself to others. We recommend that you ask a person to meet with you for personal coaching and encouragement. When asked (over coffee or lunch) to support someone in leadership, nine out of ten people say, "I'd love to!" So why not ask?
- Delegate responsibilities after the first meeting. Doing so will help group members grow, and it will give you a break as well.

- Most important, cultivating your own walk with God puts you on the offensive against Satan and increases the joy zone for everyone in your life. Make a renewed decision right now to make this happen. Don't give Satan a foothold in your heart; there is simply too much at stake.

# SESSION ONE:
# GOD'S HEART FOR PEOPLE

## Goals of the Session

- To begin to see the world's lost people through the eyes and heart of God
- To identify persons in your lives who are sheep without shepherds
- To commit to some basic shared values of your group

Before you meet for the first time, invite as many people as you would enjoy hanging out with. It just makes the group a whole lot more fun for you as the leader. Also, ask one or two people if they'd be willing to colead with you so you don't have to do it alone.

*Open your meeting with a brief prayer.*

**Question 1.** As leader, you should be the first to answer this question. Your answer will model the amount of time and vulnerability you want others to imitate. If you are brief, others will be brief. If your answer is superficial, you'll set a superficial tone—but if you tell something substantive and personal, others will know that your group is a safe place to tell the truth about themselves. You might want to think about your answer ahead of time.

Be sure to give each person a chance to respond to this question, because it's an opportunity for group members to get to know each other. It's not necessary to go around the circle in order. People may have trouble limiting their answers to one minute. That's fine in a first session when everyone is getting to know each other. The CONNECTING portion of your meeting will be briefer in future sessions. If yours is a new group, it's especially important to allow extra time for people to share their personal stories. Everyone needs to feel known so that they feel they belong. The sharing of stories may decrease the available time for Bible study, but this will be time well spent in the early weeks of a group's life. And even if your group has been meeting together for some time, you will find that the CONNECTING questions will help you understand one another better and enrich your Bible study.

**Introduction to the Series.** If this is your first study guide in the DOING LIFE TOGETHER series, you'll need to take time after question 1 to orient the group to one principle that undergirds the series: *A healthy purpose-driven small group balances the five purposes of the church in order to help people balance them in their lives.* Most small groups emphasize Bible study, fellowship, and prayer. But God has called us to reach out to others as well. If the five purposes are new to your group, be sure to review the Read Me First section with your new group. In addition, the Frequently Asked Questions section could help your group understand some of the purpose-driven group basics.

**Question 2.** If your group has done another study guide in the DOING LIFE TOGETHER series within the past six months, you may not need to go over the Purpose-Driven Group Agreement again. It's a good idea to remind people of the agreement from time to time, but for an established group, recommitting every six months is reasonable. If you're new to the series and if you don't already have a group agreement, turn to page 67 and take about ten minutes to look at the Purpose-Driven Group Agreement. Read each value aloud in turn, and let group members comment at the end. Emphasize confidentiality—a commitment that is essential to the ability to trust each other.

"Spiritual Health" says that group members give permission to encourage each other to set spiritual goals *for themselves.* As the study progresses, a group member may set a goal to do daily devotions, or a dad may set a goal to spend half an hour each evening with his children. No one will set goals for someone else; each person will be free to set his or her own goals.

Regarding expectations: It's amazing how many groups never take the time to make explicit plans about refreshments, child care, and other such issues. Child care is a big issue in many groups. It's important to treat it as an issue that the group as a whole needs to solve, even if the group decides that each member will make arrangements separately.

If you feel that your group needs to move on, you can save the conversation about expectations until the end of your meeting.

**Question 3.** Have someone read the Bible passage aloud. It's a good idea to ask someone ahead of time, because not everyone is comfortable reading aloud in public. When the passage has been read, ask question 3. Don't be afraid to allow silence while people think. It's completely normal to have periods of silence in a Bible study. You might count to seven silently. If nobody says anything, say something humorous like, "I can wait longer than you can!" It's not necessary that everyone respond to every one of the Bible study questions.

**Questions 4–5.** Jesus saw people's physical, political, and spiritual needs. He knew that many were poor. He knew that the Roman army was oppressing them. And he knew that they were messing up their lives by not obeying God. He knew that they were confused about what God was like and what kind of relationship God wanted to have with them. He cared about all their needs and understood that they needed intensive, ongoing shepherding to address all those needs. They needed to know and follow him as their good shepherd.

**Question 6.** Multitudes of people need to know Jesus as the good shepherd, but far too few of those who know him are helping others come to know him.

**Question 7.** It's common for Christians to feel angry, frustrated, or even indifferent toward those who don't seem to want Jesus as their shepherd. Compassion grows as we allow ourselves to see these people as Jesus sees them. If group members are reluctant to own up to their genuine feelings toward unbelievers, you can set an example by sharing your honest feelings about an unbeliever in your life.

**Question 9.** Two obstacles are *busyness* and *fear*. Some of us are too busy caring for ourselves and our families to care about people who don't know Jesus. Some of us fear the humiliation we might feel if someone rejected our beliefs about Jesus. (What if I sound foolish? What if I don't know how to explain the gospel well enough?) Or perhaps we fear offending people. Talk about these obstacles and how they might be addressed and overcome.

**Questions 10–11.** Praying for people is a great way to cultivate compassion for them. As you pray for them, you'll begin to see needs in their lives that the gospel addresses. Give people about a minute to write names in the circles, then gather a name or two from each person to form the group's Top Ten list.

**Question 12.** The devotional passages on page 81 give your group a chance to test-drive the spiritual discipline of spending daily time with God. Encourage everyone to give it a try. There are five short readings for each session, so people can read one a day and even skip a couple of days a week. Talk to your group about committing to reading and reflecting on these verses each day. This practice has revolutionized the spiritual lives of others who have used this study, so we highly recommend it. There will be an opportunity in future sessions to share what you have discovered in your devotional reading. Remind group members of the sample journal page on page 84.

Beginning in session 2, people will have an opportunity to check in with one other member at the end of several of the group sessions to share what they learned from the Lord in their devotional time.

Consider giving one or more group members the chance to be a facilitator for a meeting. Healthy groups rotate their leadership each week. No one person has to carry all the responsibility. What's more, it helps develop everyone's gifts in a safe environment, and, best of all, you learn different things through the eyes of different people with different styles. You can use the Small Group Calendar (page 69) to help manage your rotating schedule.

## Goals of the Session

- To learn to notice and respond to people's real needs
- To set a personal goal in the area of faith sharing

New rotating leaders may want to meet ahead of time with an experienced leader to review the plan for the meeting. You may want to have some extra booklets on hand for any new group members.

**Question 1.** Think ahead of time about what you needed when you came to faith in Jesus. Try to use plain language in speaking of your needs, with as little psychological or theological jargon as possible. Talk about a need you were aware of (a felt need) and perhaps also a deeper need you may not have been aware of. Maybe your life seemed meaningless, and you felt a need to become part of something larger than yourself. Maybe you knew you needed freedom from an addiction. Maybe you were a child and felt a need to belong to your family's faith community. These are all felt needs—and legitimate ones as well. Of course, you also needed forgiveness of sins, a relationship with God, and eternal life. These are deeper needs. Most people come to Jesus to meet a mixture of needs they're only partly aware of. Discussing question 1 will help group members begin to think about needs—for some this may be the first time they've ever thought about needs.

**Question 2.** Jesus initiated this relationship by putting himself in the humble position of one who has needs. He needed water, and he asked a stranger—a woman and a Samaritan, no less—for it. He could easily have been rejected. Asking someone for something you need says, "I respect you, and I'm not afraid to admit that you have something I need." Many a relationship has begun when a neighbor asked to borrow another neighbor's shovel. Jesus neither whined nor demanded; he simply asked.

**Question 4.** The woman thought she needed physical water. Jesus knew she needed respect, kindness, and forgiveness for her life's failures—and ultimately a connection with the Messiah. She may very well have rejected someone who offered solutions for her spiritual needs (forgiveness, a Messiah) without showing respect and kindness first. Jesus moved into her life gently but firmly, slowly peeling away layers of her defenses.

**Questions 11–12.** If group members have never taken the Purpose-Driven Life Health Assessment or set a goal for their spiritual lives, it's worth taking ten or fifteen minutes to do this. Setting a goal in the area of faith sharing is scary for many people. They may be painfully aware of falling far short in this area of life, yet busyness and fear are strong barriers to change.

Familiarize yourself with the Purpose-Driven Life Health Assessment before the meeting. You may want to take the assessment yourself ahead of time and think about your goal. Then you can give group members a real-life example of what you are actually committed to doing. We also encourage you to complete a simple goal under each purpose. Ask your coleader or a trusted friend to review it with you. Then you'll understand the power of this tool and the support you can gain from a spiritual partner.

Offer the health assessment in a spirit of grace. It should make people hungry to see the Holy Spirit work in their lives, not ashamed that they're falling short. Nobody can do these things in the power of the flesh! And sometimes the most mature believers have the clearest perception of the areas in which they need considerable help from the Spirit.

Help guide group members to pair up with partners with whom they will have a good chemistry. Spiritual partnership works best when people trust each other. Point out the Spiritual Partners' Check-In Page on page 77, which can give partners a structure for checking in with each other. Bear in mind that some personalities love self-assessments and setting goals, while others are more resistant. Some people who routinely set goals at work may be taken aback at the idea of setting a goal for their spiritual lives. Assure everyone that their goals can be small steps, that no one will be pressured into performing or humiliated for falling short, and that God is always eager to give grace.

The Purpose-Driven Life Health Plan on pages 74–76 is a tool to help people be more focused in setting goals for spiritual health. It contains suggested goals, questions to think about, and a chart for keeping track of feedback from spiritual partners. Point it out and encourage group members to use it if it seems helpful. You may also want to consult your Small Group Calendar (page 69) to see who might lead your discussion next time.

# SESSION THREE: BUILDING BRIDGES THROUGH RELATIONSHIPS

## Goals of the Session

- To see the importance of building relationships with unbelievers
- To practice telling bite-sized pieces of your faith story that unbelievers can relate to

**Question 1.** Busyness is the number-one reason many Christians have no non-Christian friends. You can set an example by thinking through the times in a typical week when you encounter non-Christians naturally.

**Question 2.** Being a servant is a lot like being a friend. You can take an interest in people's lives, offer to baby-sit their kids (and let them baby-sit yours some other time), help them with a house project, assist a coworker with a thorny work problem, and so on.

**Questions 3–4.** Becoming a servant to unbelievers costs time and energy. Sometimes it costs emotional grief when people hurt you. The costs are worthwhile if you conclude that one of the core purposes of your life is to extend God's love to unbelievers. If this purpose isn't profoundly important to you, then you probably won't make the effort. The costs are also worthwhile if you think you have a reasonable chance of making a difference in someone's life. If you expect to fail or be rejected, you very likely won't make the effort. Allow group members to be honest about their fears of failure and about their competing priorities. Guilt doesn't make people effective evangelists over the long haul. People need to face and overcome their fears. They need to be motivated by love for others.

**Question 5.** In 1 Corinthians 8–10, Paul guides his readers to distinguish between two kinds of situations. In one kind, the Christian is relating to sinners but is *not* tempted to copy their sin. Paul finds himself in this kind of situation frequently. He socializes with people who are sexually immoral and worship idols, but their sin doesn't appeal to him. He is able to enter their world and offer the love of Jesus without stumbling into sin. By keeping his bearings in Jesus Christ, Paul is able to show an alternative lifestyle that is attractive to unbelievers.

In the other kind of situation, the Christian is relating to sinners and *is* tempted to copy their sin. For example, a man is invited to a strip club, but he knows he can't go there without being unfaithful to his wife in his thoughts. Throughout 1 Corinthians 10, Paul tells the Corinthians to say no to situations like this. Christians need to know their own weak spots and draw their boundaries accordingly.

**Question 8.** Teaming up with other Christians to make friends with non-Christians is a great way to approach the challenge of sharing your faith. A team approach reduces fears of rejection and strengthens the example you set for others. People are drawn to Christians who genuinely care for each other and don't need to commit sin in order to have fun. If you and another group member share an interest in a sport or hobby, maybe you know an unbeliever who likes the same thing and would enjoy participating with you. In session 6 you'll have a chance to talk about hosting a group party and inviting your non-Christian friends.

## Goals of this Session

- To be encouraged to make the most of opportunities in your relationships with non-Christians
- To learn how to talk about your experience of Christian faith in ways outsiders can relate to

**Question 4.** It's wise, for example, to behave with integrity and kindness, even when others don't (1 Peter 2:19). If we want to win a hearing for the gospel, we'll need to excel at relationships and integrity.

**Question 5.** Grace-full conversation is generous and comes after much listening to the other person. We don't just press our own opinions. Grace-full persons find ways of talking about their moral standards in ways that are clear, yet respectful. They avoid sarcasm and stereotyping when critiquing the moral standards of others.

**Question 6.** We might say, "That's a good question, and I don't know a good answer. But I can talk to somebody and get back to you." Or, "This wasn't an issue when I came to faith in Christ, so I don't know much about it. But I can ask someone and get back to you." There's nothing wrong with admitting that you don't know. It's humility, not humiliation. Afterward, we might read a book or article on the subject or ask our pastor or our small group members for their thoughts.

**Question 8.** Don't underestimate the power of this exercise. Here you are putting your Bible study into practice. One of the main reasons people give for not talking about their faith is not knowing what to say. This four-step outline will help them figure out what to say.

The footnotes guide those who don't have a classic story of adult conversion. Christians are often reluctant to tell unbelievers about their struggles against sin because they think that their struggles will make them—or Jesus—look bad. In reality, unbelievers who are becoming aware of their own struggles in life are drawn to Christians who admit that they also struggle. Unbelievers who think that their lives are great are generally closed to the gospel—they're not the ones to whom you'll be revealing your struggles. It's the unbelievers who are *dissatisfied* with their lives who are potentially open to the touch of Jesus. They may well be delighted to talk to a Christian who has faced anxiety over money, or marital stress, or career uncertainty, or personal failure—and has overcome the adversity by God's grace. They will not be put off if you admit to having struggled with arrogance or selfishness or fear. Quite the contrary. The key is that you have been arrogant or selfish or scared—*and you've been changed*. This is what is so rare in the world.

An added benefit of this exercise is that group members get to hear each other's stories. Sharing these stories with each other will draw your group together in astonishing ways. Encourage people not to sugarcoat their stories. It's not necessary to have an issue all tied up with ribbons at the end of a story. For example, if your story is about anger, it's fine if you're *still* struggling with anger at someone while God is gradually softening your heart. Genuineness is what draws unbelievers—they can detect pretense a mile away.

Encourage people to write out as homework their stories in all four areas.

# SESSION FIVE: EXPLAINING THE GOSPEL

## Goals of the Session

- To learn how to share the gospel with a non-Christian
- To overcome fears about sharing the gospel

**Question 1.** To *propitiate* someone is to do something to turn aside his or her wrath. "Christ propitiated God in the sense that he turned God's wrath away from guilty sinners."* Give a round of applause to anyone who guessed right. If anyone in your group knows enough theology to debate whether Romans 3:25 is really about propitiation or about expiation, give that person a double round of applause, but ask him to save the debate for another time. Whew!

**Question 2.** Peter says that people are unlikely to hurt us if we treat them well and share the gospel with them respectfully. And, he says, even if they do, it's not the end of the world. The prospect of being hurt doesn't scare Peter the way it scares many of us. Group members may respond, "Well, it *does* scare me!" or, "What does Peter have that makes him shrug off rejection?" By exploring their own responses, group members can overcome their fears.

**Question 3.** Many people think that contentment means not wanting anything they don't have. But what attracts unbelievers is *hope*—wanting more than this life offers, groaning honestly while we wait, and living bold and generous lives because we know that disappointment is not the last word. True contentment is trusting God and loving others—even while we don't have what we want.

**Question 5.** The hard parts of the gospel to explain to unchurched people are "saved," "died for our sins," and the historical fact of the resurrection. The study notes will help you put these ideas into your own words. The Bridge to Life (question 7) will also help. Take some time to talk about these ideas until people really understand them. It's remarkable how many Christians are vague about what sin is and are largely unaware of their own sin.

---

*J. D. Douglas and Merrill C. Tenney, "Propitiation," *The New International Dictionary of the Bible* (Grand Rapids: Zondervan, 1987), 828.

Non-Christians are often completely unaware of doing anything that's bad enough to need someone to die for them. The kind of sexual naughtiness that most people think of as "sin," for example, just doesn't seem a big enough deal to require a crucifixion or burning in hell. You might want to talk about sins like arrogance, apathy toward others' suffering, and indifference toward God.

If people are confused about the resurrection, the rest of 1 Corinthians 15 explains it. Resurrection is not the mere resuscitation of a corpse; the risen body is different in composition from our natural bodies. Yet resurrection involves bodies—not just some ethereal "spiritual" life for disembodied souls.

**Question 7.** Take time before your meeting to read through the Bridge to Life and draw it for yourself. It will be helpful if you walk group members through the process of drawing the Bridge while explaining each step. It's easier for people to learn to use the Bridge if someone shows them how. After you show them, give time to practice with each other. Let them know that the Bridge is available as a small tract, which they can take with them when they sit down with an unbeliever.

Here is a rough script for sharing the Bridge with someone:

*Step 1.* On the left side of your page, draw a straight line with a person standing on it. (The person can be a stick figure.) Say, "God created us in his own image to be his friend and to experience a full life, assured of his love, abundant and eternal. Jesus said, 'I have come that they may have life, and have it to the full.' But if God planned for us to have peace and abundant life right now, why are most people not having this experience?"

*Step 2.* From the straight line you've drawn, draw downward the side of a cliff. Draw a similar cliff on the right side of your page. In between is a chasm. Under the left cliff, write, "People: Sinful." Under the right cliff write, "God: Holy." Say, "God created us to be able to have real relationships, the way he has relationships. He wanted us to be able to love, and this includes the freedom to choose not to love. He didn't make us robots who would automatically love and obey him. He gave us a will and a freedom to choose. We chose to disobey God and go our own willful way. We still make this choice today, which results in separation from God. The Bible says, 'For all have sinned and fall short of the glory of God.' Sin is choosing not to treat God or other people with love. Sin is also the ingrained hard-heartedness we all have that makes us unable to love perfectly, even when we want to. On our own there's no way we can attain the perfect love we need in order to bridge the gap to God. Throughout the centuries, people have tried many ways—without success. Good works won't do it—or religion, or money, or morality, or philosophy, or . . . Trying hard to love God doesn't work. We can never clean up our act enough to pay for all the loving things we've failed to do."

*Step 3.* Draw a cross that bridges the chasm between the two cliffs. Say, "Jesus Christ is the only answer to this problem. He died on the cross and rose from the grave, paying the penalty for our sin and bridging the gap between God and people. The Bible says, 'For Christ died for sins once for all, the righteous for the unrighteous, to bring you to God.' Jesus Christ paid with his life for all our past failures. He also paid to make it possible for us to love in ways we could not do on our own. And if we ever doubt that God loves us, we can remember that Jesus, the Son of God, was willing to die for us."

*Step 4.* Say, "Believing in Jesus means trust and commitment. It means acknowledging our sinfulness, trusting Jesus' forgiveness, and letting him rule our life. Eternal, abundant life is a gift for us to receive. The Bible says, 'For God so loved the world that he gave his one and only Son, that whoever believes in him shall not perish but have eternal life.'"

Ask your friend, "Where would you draw yourself in this illustration?" Allow your friend to point to the spot and explain why he chose that spot. If he thinks he's on God's side, ask him some questions to be sure he understands what it means to be on God's side. You might ask, for example, "How important is Jesus Christ in your life?" If he thinks he's on the sin side of the chasm, ask, "Is there any reason that would keep you from crossing over to God's side and being certain of eternal life?" and, "What is keeping you from inviting Jesus into your life and crossing the bridge to a relationship with God?" If he wants to do so, lead him through the steps of receiving Jesus Christ. If he wants time to think about it, tell him it's fine for him to do so. Invite him to keep the drawing of the two cliffs and the cross. If he says, "No thanks," be sure to affirm that you're not ending your friendship over this issue. It's very important that a person know you value him—whether or not he receives Christ.

**Question 10.** You might want to check with your church leaders to make sure they're comfortable with small groups sharing Communion together. If they are, you'll find it a rewarding experience.

## Goals of the Session

- To understand that sharing your faith includes helping younger believers grow from spiritual infancy to maturity
- To agree on a plan to reach out as a group to unbelievers
- To celebrate the completion of this study

**Questions 1-2.** You should be the first to give your responses here. Think about your answers ahead of time so you can share something genuine, substantive, and warm. You'll set the tone for everyone else. It's important not to be superficial or too general when affirming your group's strengths. Thinking ahead will also help you keep your response concise so that others will try to be concise as well.

**Question 3.** Go. Make disciples of all nations. Baptize them in the name of the Father, Son, and Holy Spirit. Teach them to obey everything Jesus commanded. No small task!

**Question 6.** Matthew's gospel is full of Jesus' commands, so it's a good place to start looking. The Sermon on the Mount (Matthew 5–7) will keep anyone busy for a while. The other gospels, and ultimately the rest of the New Testament, fill out the picture of Jesus' commands. And of course the Old Testament laws and stories shed light on the New Testament way of life that Jesus (a practicing Jew whose only Bible was the Old Testament) taught.

**Question 7.** If making friends with our non-Christian neighbors feels like a stretch, reaching out to people from other cultures will be even more so. This question is meant to broaden awareness, not apply pressure. Think about what your group is ready for.

**Question 9.** If you have time for nothing else, do make a plan to reach out as a team. You'll be far more effective if outsiders can see the life you're experiencing together, and you'll be far less vulnerable to fear, discouragement, and distraction.

**Question 10.** Be sure to reserve ten minutes to review your Purpose-Driven Group Agreement. The end of a study is a chance to evaluate what has been good and what could be improved on in your group. It's a time for some people to bow out gracefully and for others to recommit for a new season. If you're planning to go on to another study in the DOING LIFE TOGETHER series, session 1 of that study will reintroduce the agreement. You don't have to discuss it again then if you do so now.

Consider planning a celebration to mark the end of this episode in your group. You might share a meal, go out for dessert, or plan a party for your next meeting.

# SMALL GROUP ROSTER

| Name | Address | Phone | E-mail Address | Team or Role | Church Ministry |
|------|---------|-------|----------------|--------------|-----------------|
| Bill Jones | 7 Almlar Street L.F. 92665 | 766-2255 | bjones@aol.com | Socials | children's ministry |
| | | | | | |
| | | | | | |
| | | | | | |
| | | | | | |
| | | | | | |
| | | | | | |
| | | | | | |
| | | | | | |

Be sure to pass your booklets around the room the first night, or have someone volunteer to type the group roster for all members. Encourage group ownership by having each member share a team role or responsibility.

| Name | Address | Phone | E-mail Address | Team or Role | Church Ministry |
|---|---|---|---|---|---|
|  |  |  |  |  |  |
|  |  |  |  |  |  |
|  |  |  |  |  |  |
|  |  |  |  |  |  |
|  |  |  |  |  |  |
|  |  |  |  |  |  |
|  |  |  |  |  |  |
|  |  |  |  |  |  |
|  |  |  |  |  |  |
|  |  |  |  |  |  |

# ABOUT THE AUTHORS

**Brett and Dee Eastman** have served at Saddleback Valley Community Church since July 1997, after previously serving for five years at Willow Creek Community Church in Illinois. Brett's primary responsibilities are in the areas of small groups, strategic planning, and leadership development. Brett has earned his Masters of Divinity degree from Talbot School of Theology and his Management Certificate from Kellogg School of Business at Northwestern University. Dee is the real hero in the family, who, after giving birth to Joshua and Breanna, gave birth to identical triplets—Meagan, Melody, and Michelle. Dee is the coleader of the women's Bible study at Saddleback Church called "The Journey." They live in Las Flores, California.

**Todd and Denise Wendorff** have served at Saddleback Valley Community Church since 1998. Todd is a pastor in the Maturity Department at Saddleback, and Denise coleads a women's Bible class with Dee Eastman called "The Journey." Todd earned a Masters of Theology degree from Talbot School of Theology. He has taught Biblical Studies courses at Biola University, Golden Gate Seminary, and other universities. Previously, Todd and Denise served at Willow Creek Community Church. They love to help others learn to dig into God's Word for themselves and experience biblical truths in their lives. Todd and Denise live in Trabuco Canyon, California, with their three children, Brooke, Brittany, and Brandon.

**Karen Lee-Thorp** has written or cowritten more than fifty books, workbooks, and Bible studies. Her books include *A Compact Guide to the Christian Life*, *How to Ask Great Questions*, and *Why Beauty Matters*. She was a senior editor at NavPress for many years and series editor for the LifeChange Bible study series. She is now a freelance writer living in Brea, California, with her husband, Greg Herr, and their daughters, Megan and Marissa.

# DOING LIFE TOGETHER SERIES

### Brett & Dee Eastman; Karen Lee-Thorp; Denise & Todd Wendorf

With six sessions in each volume, the Doing Life Together Series provides small group members with basic training on how to live healthy and balanced lives—purpose driven lives.

Based on the five biblical purposes that form the bedrock of Saddleback Church, Doing Life Together is a comprehensive study of the Purpose-Driven® Life. It will help you cultivate a healthy, balanced Christian Life together with a friend, small group or even your entire church. This experienced team of writers will take you on a spiritual journey, discovering not only what God created you for but also how you can turn that dream into an everyday reality. Experience the transformation first-hand as you Begin, Connect, Grow, Develop, Share, and Surrender your life together for him.

"Doing Life Together is a groundbreaking study...[It's] the first small group curriculum built completely on the purpose-driven paradigm...The greatest reason I'm excited about [it] is that I've seen the dramatic changes it produces in the lives of those who study it."

—From the foreword by Rick Warren

**Softcover**

*Beginning Life Together* ISBN: 0-310-24672-5

*Connecting with God's Family* ISBN: 0-310-24673-3

*Growing to Be Like Christ* ISBN: 0-310-24674-1

*Developing Your SHAPE to Serve Others* ISBN: 0-310-24675-X

*Sharing Your Life Mission Every Day* ISBN: 0-310-24676-8

*Surrendering Your Life for God's Pleasure* ISBN: 0-310-24677-6

ZONDERVAN™

GRAND RAPIDS, MICHIGAN 49530

WWW.ZONDERVAN.COM

www.lifetogether.com

Pick up a copy at your favorite bookstore today!

**Look for accompanying DVD's coming in the summer of 2003!**

# The Purpose-Driven® Life
WHAT ON EARTH AM I HERE FOR?

RICK WARREN

The most basic question everyone faces in life is *Why am I here? What is my purpose?* Self-help books suggest that people should look within, at their own desires and dreams, but Rick Warren says the starting place must be with God — and his eternal purposes for each life. Real meaning and significance comes from understanding and fulfilling God's purposes for putting us on earth.

*The Purpose-Driven Life* takes the groundbreaking message of the award-winning *Purpose-Driven Church* and goes deeper, applying it to the lifestyle of individual Christians. This book helps readers understand God's incredible plan for their lives. Warren enables them to see "the big picture" of what life is all about and begin to live the life God created them to live.

*The Purpose-Driven Life* is a manifesto for Christian living in the 21st century — a lifestyle based on eternal purposes, not cultural values. Using biblical stories and letting the Bible speak for itself, Warren clearly explains God's 5 purposes for each of us:

We were planned for God's pleasure — experience real worship.
We were formed for God's family — enjoy real fellowship.
We were created to become like Christ — learn real discipleship.
We were shaped for serving God — practice real ministry.
We were made for a mission — live out real evangelism.

This long-anticipated book is the life-message of Rick Warren, founding pastor of Saddleback Church. Written in a captivating devotional style, the book is divided into 40 short chapters that can be read as a daily devotional, studied by small groups, and used by churches participating in the nationwide "40 Days of Purpose" campaign (Fall, 2002).

Hardcover: 0-310-20571-9          Unabridged Audio Pages® CD: 0-310-24788-8
Unabridged Audio Pages® cassette: 0-310-20907-2

## Also available from Inspirio, the gift division of Zondervan

| | |
|---|---|
| Purpose-Driven Life Journal: | 0-310-80306-3 |
| What on Earth Am I Here For? (Mass Market): | 0-310-80324-1 |
| Planned for God's Pleasure (Gift Book): | 0-310-80322-5 |
| Scripture Keeper Plus Purpose-Driven® Life: | 0-310-80323-3 |